TRUGANINNI INSIDE OUT

First published in 2016 by Reed Independent, Victoria, Australia.

Printed by Createspace.com, a division of Amazon.com.

Available as a printed book or an ebook from Createspace.com or Amazon.com
or Kindle estores, together with most major international online outlets or
bookshops with online ordering facilities:
paperback: ISBN 9780994531148
ebook: ISBN 9780994531155

Front cover: Dilani Priyangika Ranaweera, Dart Lanka Productions, Sri Lanka

National Library of Australia Cataloguing-in-Publication entry:
Creator: Reed, Bill, author.
Title: Truganinni Inside Out/ Bill Reed
Edition: first
ISBN: 9780994531148 (paperback)
ISBN: 9780994531155 (ebook)
Notes: includes bibliographical reference.
Subjects: Drama/indigenous/black comedy
Dewey Number: A822.3

TRUGANINNI INSIDE OUT

a play

Bill Reed

R

Also by Bill Reed
Plays
Burke's Company
Bullsh/ More Bullsh
Cass Butcher Bunting
Mr Siggie Morrison with his Comb and Paper
Truganinni
Living in Black Holes (anthology)
Living on Mars (anthology)
Living on Mars: the play
Daddy the 8th
Truganinni Inside Out
Auntie and the Girl
Mirror, Mirror
Little She
You Want It, Don't You, Billy?
The Pecking Order
Jack Charles is Up and Fighting
Just Out of Your Ground
I Don't Know What to Do with You!
Paddlesteamer

novels
The Pipwink Papers\
Me, the Old Man
Stigmata
Ihe
Dogod
Crooks
Tusk
Throw her back
Are You Human?
Tasker Tusker Tasker
Awash
1001 Lankan Nights book 1
1001 Lankan Nights book 2
Passing Strange

Nonfiction
Water Workout

Award-winning short stories (see also title 'Passing Strange')
Messman on the C.E. Altar
The 200-year Old Feet
The Case Inside
Blind Freddie Among the Pickle Jars
The Old Ex-serviceman
The Shades of You my Dandenong

Selected and now listed on the Australian Script Centre's website Australianplays.org.

As its earlier shape, titled 'Truganinni Inside', this piece was listed for active production consideration by the Melbourne Theatre Company in 2004. In regard to this, Dr Julian Meyrick, the Director of the MTC, wrote on10 November of that year:

'I enjoyed the play immensely. The great strength of the writing, to my mind, is the way you handle the indigenous characters. So often this is not the case, and the results are stereotypes or caricatures on stage. But Truganinni and Nanna live powerfully. When Nanna, Truganinni and McKay tell Truganinni's story together it is unforgettable. Truganinni's cry… "What I remember does not happen any more"– contains a depth of loss that has no end to it, it seems…'

The Backgrounds

King Billy (William Lanne)

King Billy (real name William Lanne) died in 1869 at the age of 34. As the 'last' male Tasmanian, his skeleton was valuable. After death, they removed his skull from its skin; cut off his hands, cut off his feet, grave-robbed him. His fully-identified bones were never found.

He was best known as the last full-blooded Aboriginal Tasmanian man.

He was captured along with his family in 1842 during a period known as the Black War. He was the youngest child in the last family taken to the Aboriginal camp at Wybelenna on Flinders Island by George Augustus Robinson. His native name is lost.

In 1855 he joined a whaling ship and regularly visited Oyster Cove when he had time. Lanne died on 3 March 1869 from a combination of cholera and dysentery.

Following his death, his body was dismembered and used for scientific purposes. A member of the English College of Surgeons named William Crowther managed to break into the morgue where King Billy's body was and decapitated the corpse, removed the skin and inserted a skull from a white body into the black skin. The Tasmanian Royal Society soon discovered Crowther's work, and decided to thwart any further attempts to collect "samples" by amputating the hands and feet. Lanne was then buried in this state.

Because he was accused of the theft of Lanney's head (and the illicit use of another white person's head!), Crowther's honorary appointment as surgeon at the Colonial Hospital terminated. Yet in 1869, the Council of the Royal College of Surgeons awarded him a gold medal and the first Fellowship of the College ever awarded to an Australian. Crowther later became Premier of Tasmania. Crowther claimed that, because Lanne had lived much of his life within the European community, his brain had exhibited physical changes, demonstrating "the improvement that takes place in the lower race when subjected to the effects of education and civilisation."

Although it is not known for certain what happened to the stolen remains of Lanne... several bodies of Crowther's collection were donated to the anatomy department at the University of Edinburgh. In the 1990s, the Tasmanian Aboriginal Centre believed Lanney's skull to be among them, and requested their return. The remains were ultimately returned and reburied, though the university officially denied that the remains belonged to Lanne.
Wikipedia

Truganinni
'She was the daughter of Mangana, Chief of Bruni Island. Later in life, when she had mastered English, she told her story to Alexander McKay. Her mother was stabbed to death by a European. Her sister was carried off by sealers. In her childhood, accompanied by her intended husband Paraweena and another man, she was once on the mainland of Van Diemans Land. Two sawyers, Lowe and Newell, undertook to row the party to nearby Bruni Island. In mid-channel, the white men threw the natives overboard. As they struggled and grasped the gunwale, Lowe and Newell chopped off their hands with hatchets. The mutilated Aborigines were left to drown and the Europeans were free to do as they pleased with the girl.'
Clive Turnbull, 'The Black War'

'... For example, the Tasmanian Aborigines died out not just because they were hunted like kangaroos for an afternoon's sport, but also because a world in which this could happen was intolerable to them; so they committed suicide as a race by refusing to breed. Ironically perhaps, and as though to confirm the Aborigines' judgement, the mummified remains of the old lady who was the last to survive have been preserved as a museum curiosity.'
A. A. Alvarez, 'The Savage God'

'Seven years after King Billy's death, Truganinni stood alone, a living relic of her race.   She would walk the streets of Hobart Town, resembling Queen Victoria in her voluminous skirts and headdress.   She quite enjoyed the curiosity and finger pointing of the townspeople.

Towards the end, she appeared to bear no malice towards her race's persecutors.   Growing stoutish, she smoked a pipe and enjoyed a daily jug of beer.   But she began to grow ill and as her death loomed, so did the memories of what happened to King Billy's body.

The fear obsessed her like a disease and repeatedly she begged and pleaded that no such horror should befall her.

On May 8th 1876, at the approximate age of 73, Truganinni died. Only hours after the news, body-snatchers in the Royal Society of Tasmania started to bark for her body.   The government tried to fight them off.   She was buried in a secret grave in a plain wooden casket. But the promises made to her were false ones, yet again. Years after her death her body was exhumed with the full approval of the government.   Her skeleton was displayed in the Tasmanian Museum, alongside the skeletons of animals.

In 1953, a deputation to the Tasmanian Premier resulted in her skeleton being removed from public display and placed in a box to be opened only by 'bona fide' scientists.

And thus, for decades and in a black casket in Hobart's Tasmanian Museum, lay the broken bones of an aboriginal queen – and in her irreverent tomb are squashed the broken dreams of a race.'
Tess Lawrence, Melbourne Herald

Author's note*:*   In 2002, there came an official public burial of sorts. Some of her 'hair and flesh' that had been lodged with the College of Surgeons in London were returned to Tasmania, allowing a formal ceremony before the nation's cameras of scattering her ashes on the waters of her beloved Derwent.

9

The Characters

This is a play for six characters only. It is set in three parts, and each part uses some, not all, of the following 'pool' of characters:

TRUGANINNI
is maybe 15 years for the first Act; 55 or so for the second Act; and 73 for Act three.

NANNA
the quarter-caste housekeeper to George Augustus Robinson, the most successful of the religious 'conciliators' of the Van Diemens Land. Nanna is all bones but all brawn; and the real energy in her companionship of Truganinni. At first she is around 30, rising through the stages to be 78 or so… but she always seemed to be going on a 100.

ALEXANDER McKAY
at first stage, the young adherent/assistant to Robinson but kindly and confused where Robinson was crude and self-seeking. McKay is to become the first relater of Truganinni's story. Initially, he is in the making of the damaging, pompous do-gooder he is to become. When we meet him later in the play, he has obviously done well out of being associated with the Reverend Robinson. He is now a leading authority on the Tasmanian Aborigines.

WILLIAM CROWTHER
visiting medical advisor to the Mission on Flinders Island, appointed through the influences of the Royal College of Surgeons in London to keep a close eye on the Tasmanians for their 'anthropological value'. He will become Premier of Tasmania but will think it nothing to sneak in at night, lift King Billy out of his coffin, remove his skull and replace it with another skull from some other (White, this time) body. About his oath to humanity as a doctor, he would only remember he had taken it if he were truthful, which it is not. Self-satisfied and loud cynicism.

BARNETT LEVEY
entrepreneur, louder waist-coated than he even was in Cockney
London. Started Sydney's famous Royal Theatre, though, and put
on the better early extravaganzas, which always began with his
own singing act. A rowdy like his audiences; grandiose, impulsive
and unrealistic, yet a true theatrical character that all recognise and
treasure. He is far more entertaining than farcical, more flippant
than callous. Life is like 'is missus… a lot of troughs.

Minor Characters:

MOLLY (*played by NANNA?*)
barmaid – that is, born on the right side of the bar. Has the
amusement that goes with observation living on that side of
Hobart wharf life.

COLVIN (*played by McKay?*)
 community undertaker but mostly whaling boat captain. A strict,
moral man, not used to being apologetic to anyone, and would
never be inclined to

ATWELL (*voiced by LEVEY*)
Colonial Under-secretary. Blood on his hands? Hardly; not even
a slip of the pen. Metaphorically, one side of his lips would turn
up, the other side down.

Act 1
King Billy Coming

(1834, the mission house of the Flinders Island settlement, established in 1831 to segregate and 'save' the few remaining survivors of the original Van Diemens Land indigenous tribes. This is the living room to the 'manse' of George Augustus Robinson, the government-appointed Chief Protector of the Tasmanian Aborigines.

Though the settlement on Flinders Island was generally rough-and-ready, this, Robinson's house, is seen as substantial. The walls are made of stone and immaculately white-washed. The furniture is of Victorian quality, and shows purposefulness and an attention to detail. It reflects the mind of Robinson; there is no self-doubt here that his mission to isolate and to civilise the Van Diemens Land Aborigines will succeed. Nor does he doubt that the atrocious weather conditions of the island will not have any bearing on this place becoming the Tasmanians permanent refuge from the whiteman's corruptive influences.

There is however a lack of grand space, as evidenced by a bed taking up a large part of the room.

This is occupied by CROWTHER, the shape covered from head to toe by the quilt. He grunts a little, turns restlessly. He is not asleep, but will be a hard man to move from there at any time.

From one of the rooms off, there is a sudden cry of annoyance, accompanied by the loud squeaking of iron bed springs and a banging of a cupboard door.

The young ALEXANDER McKAY eventually hurries into view, still trying to lace up his boots and to get his topcoat

13

on. He has to stop by the front door to finish these things.

As he does so, shadows appear in the windows to try to look in to see who is moving within. These are some of the Van Diemens Land Aborigines camped out on the verandah of the house itself. The boards start creaking out there and vague conversations start up; we sense that they too are just waking up.

Finally, fit to leave, McKAY calls back into the house)

McKAY: I'm going for the boat, if nobody else is!

(He gives up getting any acknowledgment, hurries outside. For a moment while the front door is open we glimpse the people outside on the verandah and hear his voice as he passes through them, 'Excuse me. Do you mind?'

After him and on its own, the front door swings open a little. It is pushed a little further, but whoever is doing it is reluctant to even look in too openly. Again, we hear McKAY's voice:
'That's not allowed!'
Whoever is looking in withdraws quickly. The door shuts.

For a time, there is no further movement.

Then TRUGANINNI scampers furtively in from what will prove to be the kitchen. She makes for the bookcase and whips out one of the thickest of the tomes there, an illustrated bible. Immediately engrossed in it, she shuffles backwards until her back is against the side of the bed. Once or twice she glances surreptitiously over her shoulder, but quickly returns to the book. She doesn't appear aware that she is humming loudly with contentment, counter to her attempts not to be seen or heard.

Suddenly, she is overcome with nausea and puts the book aside quickly, stands and regards the 'sleeping'

14

CROWTHER, as though he should do something. She is terribly theatrical about this – hand over mouth, hand on belly, cheeks puffed and heaving while jolting the bed. (CROWTHER, the sleeping figure still doesn't emerge from the quilt.) Yet the sickness is real and, though she makes a good attempt at getting out of the front door, she doesn't quite make it. On its threshold, she doubles over and throws up.

Note: this 'mess' will be an obstacle to all who come and go through the front door. Yet no one makes any attempt to clean it up.

Moaningly, CROWTHER gets himself up and goes to her. He helps her back to the bed, where he takes her temperature (the back of his wrist against her brow, is all) and her pulse (a couple of beats satisfy him)

CROWTHER: I should examine you properly today.

TRUGANINNI: You'll cut off my long tall Sally.

CROWTHER: From what I know about your long tall Sally, I don't think I've brought any knife sharp enough. Now, if you will excuse me…

(he pulls her unceremoniously off the bed, climbs back in himself.

Undeterred, TRUGANINNI picks up the book and returns to her reading on the floor besides the bed. She only gets away with it for a few seconds more before:)

NANNA: (from the kitchen doorway) 'Ere!

(TRUGANINNI defiantly cradles the book from her)

NANNA: That's a good book, that is.

15

TRUGANINNI: (nodding) It is the Good Book.

NANNA: You've got your naked fingers all over it, it won't be a good book for much longer. You gone deaf?

TRUGANINNI: (all innocence) What?

NANNA: The Reverend said. No books!

TRUGANINNI: He did not.

NANNA: 'Ere, I've had it with you.

> *(TRUGANINNI contemptuously turns back into the kitchen. At much the same time, NANNA notices the vomit in the doorway)*

NANNA: 'Ere, you come back here!

TRUGANINNI: What?

NANNA: You bilious all over the Reverend's rug which was there yesterday until you erked all over it when you could at least have had the decency to wait until today. You stop erking.

TRUGANINNI: Make me.

NANNA: 'Ere, the Reverend gets home this morning. You're done.
    (*then*)
Come here.

> *(Reluctantly, TRUGANINNI crosses to the older woman. NANNA grabs her with a crone's glee, but then turns gentle as she inspects TRUGANINNI's belly, teeth, back. Finally:)*

NANNA: Let me see them toes.

TRUGANINNI: (giggling) No digging up 'tatoes.

16

(Eventually satisfied with the toes, NANNA mock-reels at the smell of her fingers, mock-fights with TRUGANINNI to try to put her fingers under her nose, and finally leaves for the kitchen.

For a brief moment, TRUGANINNI is tempted to go for the book again)

CROWTHER: (from under the covers) If you must do that again, please turn the pages quietly.

(Anyway, she is stopped short by NANNA reappearing angrily)

NANNA: 'Ere, I've had it with you. Where's the water on?

TRUGANINNI: Gotta go to the lav.

NANNA: You keep your hole away from the lav!
    (*indicating the Aborigines outside*)
You go out and use the nearest bush. You think you're better'n our own people?

TRUGANINNI: (scandalized) I'm inside!

NANNA: We'll see about that when the Reverend gets back.

TRUGANINNI: (lecherous hand miming) Reverend. Reverend Grabgrabgrab.
    (*indicates the veranda outside*)
I'd be better off out there with them.

(NANNA crosses surprisingly quickly to slap her hard)

NANNA: They're sick as dogs out there!
    (*quickly apologetic*)
'Ere, you don't get that water on, you get the boot outside.
Blurting, always blurting out something, you are.

17

(She leaves for the kitchen.

TRUGANINNI prods CROWTHER and goes self-pityingly:)

TRUGANINNI: Sir! You help? I'm inside. You tell her.

(CROWTHER refuses to react to her, even though she gives him the long stare.

Finally she gives up, makes a rude face to the 'lump' of him and then moves into another room and returns immediately with a broom and pan. She goes to clean up the mess by the door, but is interrupted by McKAY returning. He is visibly upset, backs in apologizing to the people on the veranda, inadvertently avoids the vomit by inches, takes the broom and pan from her, opens door, hands it to someone outside. Then realizes what he has done and opens the door again, grabs back the broom and pan and returns it to TRUGANINNI, who shrugs, as any lazy domestic would given half the hint that the job doesn't have to be done, and relegates them to the nearest corner.

Mindless of this, McKAY talks in CROWTHER's general direction, but not necessarily at him:)

McKAY: I missed Robinson. How could I know there were at least five other passengers getting off? Good grief, it's only a whaler. I'm trying to see him but they're all getting on and getting off and getting on and getting off and getting on and getting off. Well, off, anyway, when they're not getting on and getting off.

(Tapping on the window outside saves CROWTHER from having to answer. McKAY crosses, sees it is 'only' the Aborigines and shouts:)

McKAY: I'm surviving on an empty stomach too, you know!
    (listens and throws disgustedly in CROWTHER's direction)

18

Now they're demanding where's last night's dinner is! How can one possibly keep up with them? Good grief!

(This time, NANNA is 'caused' to come into the room)

NANNA: I'll sew knuckles on the face of anyone cussing in this house of the Lord.

McKAY: Sorry, Nanna.

(She waves this off, crosses to open the front door, sees what she doesn't like:)

NANNA: 'Ere, who's been spilling blood? No spilling blood on the veranda! You see me coughing up in here? I bet you haven't.

(She slams the door on them)

McKAY: (needing to confess guilt) I missed your Master on the boat, Nanna.

(NANNA shrugs. McKAY sits, as though withered by her look, but jumps up to answer it, when the door knocker is used)

NANNA: (after him) Tell 'em no outside can't come in!

(She huffs out to the kitchen, diverting only to drag TRUGANINNI from the other room with her.

Before McKAY can reach the door, it is flung open and BARNETT LEVEY enters, slamming it shut behind him with his foot and making notes 'on the run', as he is doing most of the time. He deftly misses the vomit, as he barges in)

LEVEY: Venus, Hercules, Mars. Who is the genius in delving out Christian names here? I can see it in all up in lights: 'Roll up, roll up; Venus Knocks off Hercules and Mars, a Masquerade! She

Starts in on at 8 sharp!' Or, how's this? 'Extinction is Forever, Give or Take a Day!'
   (*indicating the Tasmanians outside*)
Fairly on the nosegay-garlic-spray, but, gawd, off with them petticoats and bum warmers and on with the loin cloths and a bit of girdin', and all's blooming for the professional stage if I ain't some rose bud.
   (*and at McKAY's amazed look at him*)
I know what you're thinking. Think no further, young gents.
   (*indicating CROWTHER's lump on the bed*)
Or lady and gent. Don't feel embarrassed. Who be I? Gawdluvya, if you ain't no strangers to Sydney's one'n'only Royal Theatre, then you know there's only one of yours truly. Barnett Levey, an' mighty pleased to be able to grab your bum-wipers anytime of the day or night you want to put one out.
   (*refuses McKAY's outstretched hand with theatrical flourish*)
Maybe later. Anyone for tea after all that mal de mer being belched off on the downwind? Black, only sugar, if I may say so, and I don't mind if I do. A ta for tea.

McKAY: (*managing to get his hand limply shaken*) I'm Alexander McKay, assistant to Mr Robinson. Mr Robinson is Chief Pacificator to the Natives and we...

LEVEY: Spray that 'Chief passy' again?

McKAY: Pacificator.

LEVEY: Gawdluvit. Son, you don't realize I'm a man of the theatre or you'd make that a word of one syllable, two at the top. Syllables don't fill seats, and that's me word on it. But that's enough about me. Just as important is a bob for some geezer to help Mrs Levey lug our bags up here. London to a brick, she drops to her knees after the sixth or seventh box, and it just ain't fair on the bags, ha ha.

   (*McKAY goes to introduce CROWTHER, but LEVEY hears an animal screech, and dashes to the window, looks, and calls:*)

20

LEVEY: Hoi, go easy on that tiger!
  (*watches impatiently, then yells*)
Hold that tiger! Hold that tiger!
  (*jigs to musical phrasing then stops to turn back to McKAY*)
One thing I'll say about me bread-and-strife out there… give her a
tail and she's go the cling-on no matter where it wants to take her.

McKAY: Did you say tiger?

LEVEY: Tiger, I said and tiger I'll stand by. First time I've
traveled with a tiger, son. Gawdluvher, you travel around with the
likes of Mrs Levey, you think you've had to grapple with
everything.

> (*He is mildly interrupted when CROWTHER gets up to go
> out to ablute through the kitchen door*)

McKAY: And that's Doctor Crowther, Mr Levey. Medical
advisor to the Mission on his monthly rounds. Health checks are
kept up, you know, as regular as bowels. Pardon Dr Crowther's
manner. It's been one of those times when you're up delivering
babies all night long.
  (*a confidence*)
The problem is most of the poor little wretches are born so cold.

LEVEY: Do I hear fit-to-be-laid-out dinky die dead cold cold?

McKAY: Certainly one could say very very cold. As hard as we
try to teach them otherwise, they just seem to all aim their
deliveries for the worst frosts.

LEVEY: (looking out again) Gawdluvher, that missus's got more
holds than a king's chamber pot. I could throw up a board saying
'The Bearded Lady Gives the Iddle-piddle Pussycat a Sore Nut'
and it wouldn't be far off the mark. Am I spouting the truth or
coming a cropper, or what?

NANNA: (from off) 'Ere, what's all the loud goings-on out there?

LEVEY: Who's that?

McKAY: Oh, that's only housekeeper, Nanna.

LEVEY: With a squawk like that, she'll do.

McKAY: For what?

LEVEY: Show a bit o' leg, like I your gaffer promised me, son.
  (uninvited, he looks in the kitchen, beckons)
Here you go, ladies. Fickle Fate's a'beckoning.

> *(NANNA and TRUGANINNI, unsure of themselves, tentatively do as this stranger asks. LEVEY makes himself totally at home on the bed, directs:)*

LEVEY: Stand like you'd wolf-whistle back, lovelies. Chins up. Backs straights, bellies...
  (looks)
Well, forget the bellies.
  (then)
Okay, let's see it then.

> *(He gives McKAY hand movements to begin. McKAY has no idea about what he is talking about)*

McKAY: If this is laying some sort of blame, I assure you, sir, whatever I did was inadvertent.

LEVEY: Are we ready, or am I just panting? If me drawers are drooping, call me droopy drawers.

McKAY: I don't think I'm here to make decisions about these sorts of things.

LEVEY: What sort o' things?

22

McKAY: I don't know! Whatever you've spoken to the Reverend Robinson about.

LEVEY: (no enlightenment whatsoever) These 'ere two honey-bunnies'll do for starters.

NANNA: (amazingly coquettish) You big flirt, you.

LEVEY: You little lollypop of a black-eye Susan, you.

NANNA: You're just saying that.

LEVEY: I am! Am I a sayer or a soother?

NANNA: Here, no filth in here.

LEVEY: (a romantic kidder) Am I a thinker or am I a shrinker?

NANNA: Am I a floosy or just choosy? You'll just have to wait in line.

(She elbows TRUGANINNI 'that's how you handle White men' and nearly knocks the young woman off her feet. LEVEY impatiently motions to McKAY again to get going. McKAY still has no idea of what he is supposed to do)

McKAY: Don't I remember you saying you didn't see Mr Robinson on board the boat?

LEVEY: (shrugs) Ask the missus. The moment I steps aboard, I start studying the sea at the end of me nose; that's the kind of seafarer Barnett Levey is, son. I'm a tithe man not a tide man. Let's 'ave yer, then.

(McKAY is stultified)

LEVEY: Gawdluvit, I'm talking full theatre rights 'ere, son. You don't go around just handing them in to any old quartermaster

23

unless I gander what I'm buying. I'm talking about that Catchy stuff of yours.

(and waves him impatiently on again)

McKAY: (finally) Oh, the catechisms?

LEVEY: If you say so, son.

(McKAY, giving sway to the inevitable; gives catechisms to the two women. NANNA shows all reverence; TRUGANINNI is all suppressed fury.)

McKAY: Who made you?

NANNA/TRUGANINNI: God the Father made us.

McKAY: Why did He make you?

NANNA/TRUGANINNI: So we could do His works and say 'how-do-you-do' in Heaven.

LEVEY: (interjecting) A little more leg, bit o' oomphf, son!

McKAY: How can you get to Heaven?

(This stumps them. They go as stubborn as mules.)

McKAY: (apologetically to LEVEY) The curriculum is constantly being refreshed.

(And neither is he helped by the re-emergence of CROWTHER, who proceeds to surreptitiously encourage TRUGANINNI to rebel, even as he creeps back into bed)

LEVEY: Have to say your Robinson bloke promised me lots more pace.

McKAY: (stepping it up) How can you get to Heaven?

TRUGANINNI: He said that.

NANNA: 'Ere, wash your mouth out.

McKAY: (quick repeat before it gets out of hand) How can you get to Heaven?

TRUGANINNI: (utterly rebellious) No hanging your fanny on a lamp post at night.

McKAY: That's not right.
  (swings to LEVEY and CROWTHER)
I don't want to take any blame for that.

LEVEY: (to CROWTHER) Not being a churchman m'self... what was wrong with it?

CROWTHER: Sounded reasonable to me.

LEVEY: (to TRUGANINNI) Back in Hobart Town, the Rev the Robbie the Dobbie said as how I'd gander this one here. Trinnie something or other. Always getting in the family way. But this one looks a bit done up for luck for the spotlights, old son.

McKAY: (desperately tries again) When does Jesus talk to you?!

TRUGANINNI: (a stopper) I hear Him crying in the night, longing for His home.

  (McKAY is thrown into new confusion, steps back to appeal to the others. LEVEY sucks his teeth loudly, finally turn to CROWTHER)

LEVEY: What would a know-all from the medical profession think, given that he might 'ave dispensed good coin at the box office to see this?

CROWTHER: (settling back into bed) All depends if you're offering money back.

LEVEY: There speaks the paying public, McKie the kakky. More rehearsal, son, more leg in it. You got leg garters round here? Get a few melodies goin'. It's just a question of high horses, son.

> *(There is a very long silence, while McKAY gets to understand what he means and then can get a mutual understanding with NANNA. When they do this, by head signals between them, McKAY hurries outside on the veranda and NANNA makes for the piano.*
>
> *We see McKAY's silhouette in one of the window as he, first, obviously tries to organize – with obvious great difficulty -- then 'conducts'—with obviously greater difficulty – enough of the people out there to sing.*
>
> *NANNA starts out a refrain to get them tuned in. She plays quire well. That cannot be said of her singing.*
>
> *TRUGANINNI joins her on the stool, but facing away from the piano. She sings, too, but without enthusiasm.*
>
> *They begin with Take It to the Lord in Prayer.*
>
> *It is actually not too bad, despite McKAY's problems outside. LEVEY joins in with his very-good professional voice.*
>
> *But his involvement deteriorates sharply when an animal's bark-type howling from outside starts to 'sing' along with it. This rises in discordance to dominate.*
>
> *When he hears that, LEVEY delights in shouting:)*

LEVEY: COME ON, THE TIGERS!

(Outside, McKAY gives up. signals the Tasmanians to stop. All do, including NANNA at the piano.

Eventually, there is only the howling left, and even that begins to die down, thankfully)

LEVEY: I'm goin' to change my mind about that tiger, I am. It's got possibilities, that has. Must be the missus still got hold o' its tail.

CROWTHER: Could you possibly be talking tiger like I might be talking tiger?

LEVEY: At my own personal cost, sir, barrin' a few scratches on the missus!

CROWTHER: Mr Levey, sir, hate to mention it, but there are no tigers in Van Diemans Land, sorry.

LEVEY: No tigers?! A whole zac that there one cost me, and all the halfpennies that hadn't been picked from me pocket. Mind you, that Reverend Robbie of yours might be a thieving hound but 'e did toss in the whip, I'll give him that.
    (then suspicious)
Listen 'ere, what's a beast like that got my diddly-strife's head in its mouth for, if it ain't a tiger?

CROWTHER: Van Diemen's Land, no tigers, sir.

LEVEY: All right, guv, I was saving it for the announcement. Lion.

CROWTHER: No lions neither. Sorry.

LEVEY: 'Ere, it mightn't look like a lion or a tiger to you, but people're goin' to pay good legal tender to see that tiger or lion. You just up n' take a squiz.

(beckons CROWTHER and McKAY to the window. So

27

challenged, they respond)

LEVEY: Thought somethin's a bit up, m'self. I said to the wife, I said, if this is what they call tigers down 'ere I'll be a monkey's bum, ha ha. Well, what's a man earning a honest crust to do? You tell me what's a curtain going up on Children-of-the-Wild from deep down Van Diemen's Land way wifout a wild beast or two littered around? Blimey, you must've seen a man's 'Napoleon Bonaparte' up there in Sydney if you're a man of any culture in you. Props, talk about them props. Enough horses and camels to make a right mess of the stage. Come out and I'll intruduce you to the little lady. She's the one with the paw in 'er mouth.

CROWTHER: ('no thanks') Frankly, Mr Levey, not even my Royal College of Surgeons would be interested in any skeleton of a beast that doesn't seem to be able to stand up on its own two feet. And they take anything.

LEVEY: 'Ere, four legs.

CROWTHER: Even two might be convincing.

LEVEY: So it's getting a bit long in the tooth.

CROWTHER: It has no teeth. Besides, thylacine. That's what they call them here, I believe. Van Diemen's Land wolf.

LEVEY: Tiger.

CROWTHER: Wolf.

LEVEY: Tiger, or I see my lawyer.

CROWTHER: (quickly conceding) Tiger, wolf. Wolf, tiger.

LEVEY: I see you're a man what understands the law.

CROWTHER: I am a man what understands lawyers.

LEVEY: For my 'Napoleon Bonaparte' I had an Egyptian pyramid billed as dug up from under the sandhills of South Sydney. You tell me who argues with a billboard on a little thing like a tiger or a lion?

CROWTHER: A point I might concede.

> *(They are stopped by NANNA who strides angrily back in from the kitchen, to stand nose-to-nose with CROWTHER and glares at him without talking)*

McKAY: (all innocence) Can I help you with anything, Nanna?

NANNA: 'Ere, when's the Reverend coming back to put his boot right up
> *(indicates kitchen, obviously TRUGANINNI)*
phoofphoof valve?

McKAY: All I can say is it looks like the Reverend Robinson missed the boat. He did not send me a letter, though.
> *(jealously re CROWTHER)*
He sent one to Dr Crowther.

CROWTHER: (warding him off) It is too early for reading.

LEVEY: Messy habit, ain't you right there.
> *(getting back to business with CROWTHER)*
Orright, I can't be fairer than this: you use your Royal College's maties to buy the skeleton o' my tiger out there an' I'll buy the theatre rights to this lot 'ere. Am I straight or ain't I the truth? Is it a jewish holiday or all your Christmases come at once?

CROWTHER: I am a mere physician. I have no theatre rights

LEVEY: Cos you have.

CROWTHER: Cos I haven't.

LEVEY: Lookee 'ere, can you sing?

CROWTHER: Not a whit.

LEVEY: Whistle a bit?

CROWTHER: Not a whit of a whistle, sorry. But I can act quite wittily, if I say so m'self.

LEVEY: (offended) No dirty actor in the wit business sets foot in my theatre, cocko. That sort of thing can get around.
   (*thought*)
Can you show a leg?

CROWTHER: Only a passing show.

LEVEY: Throw a good leg over?

CROWTHER: Not very passingly.

LEVEY: Got me, then.
   (*another solution*)
Tell you what, semi-dark stage, lightning outside, music up, an' you're there wif your stetho-thingoh listening to their
   (*indicates Tasmanians outside*)
 lungs all lined up...? Cough, cough. Aw, aw. Pathos, sort of thing.

CROWTHER: I could do that.

LEVEY: Well, then, you've got theatrical rights, you have!
   (*then ups the ante*)
Not cough, cough. Wheezing. No, gasping their last. Can you hold testicles and say 'wheeze your last'? Not finicky with females?

CROWTHER: Only accordingly. How much?

LEVEY: (then cunningly) For the theatrical rights? I'm only taking ten out of the sixty-four, mind.

McKAY: (waving letter) Reverend Robinson says only eight.

LEVEY: He's a thieving magpie, that Rev'rend o' yours.
 (*quickly*)
Nothing under the age o' three, neither.

McKAY: (boastfully) A few years ago, you could have picked up the theatre rights for hundreds, they were so thick on the ground.

> *(LEVEY indicates TRUGANINNI in the doorway of the kitchen.)*

LEVEY: Robbo better have included that one.

McKAY: (reaching for her, proudly) Our Truganinni. She has been with Robinson since he started.
 (*noticing the others smirking at her belly*)
I'm not responsible if someone takes that in the wrong biblical sense.
 (*but is now performing for LEVEY, turns softy to TRUGANINNI*)
Shall we tell your story, Truganinni?

> *(With surprising seriousness, she reaches up to touch his face, leads him by the hand to the couch, where she sits him down.*
>
> *NANNA will not be left out of it. She crosses to them, stands protectively by)*

McKAY: (in chant) She is called Truganinni. She is the daughter of Mangana, Chief of the Bruni Island tribe. She is a princess of her people. But her mother was stabbed to death by white men and her sister Jalmarida was carried off by sealers.

NANNA
She has gone from us;

Where has she gone?
We sit here and wait but the girl has gone.
Jalmarida is gone.

> *(NANNA moves away into shadow to sit immobile. She sits with her back to TRUGANINNI, who sways to an increasing rhythm sticks coming from outside and then approaches the seated shadow-form of her father:)*

TRUGANINNI:
Come back, father, you only sit here alone.

NANNA AS MANGANA:
At night, alone, your mother comes back to me.

TRUGANINNI:
The shadows are long. Cold winds from the north.

NANNA AS MANGANA:
The whisperings, the whisperings, the cold winds of the north.

TRUGANINNI: (outcry)
What I remember does not happen anymore!

NANNA AS MANGANA
Aiyo, where is my daughter? My daughter is gone.

TRUGANINNI:
Why do you sit here every day at my grave?
You come here and keep me warm.
For I must dance to keep myself warm.
Will you slap my loins and keep me warm?

NANNA AS MANGANA:
My wife, my daughter, I shall keep you warm.

McKAY: Halfway across the bay to Hobart town, the two whitemen threw the fiancé and the other native overboard. When they tried to hold onto the boat, they used axes to chop off their hands. She watched them drifting away, screaming for her.

TRUGANINNI: (to her 'father's' back, dry soft voice) Father, I saw them drowning, their hands floating away. One of those men was laughing. Father? My legs were not strong enough to keep them away. Father? My legs were not strong enough to keep them away. Father? They hit me, father, at both my ends.

McKAY: After they had finished with her, she was found near dead. Her father Mangana sat down in one place, and never got up. The Bruni Island tribe has now gone to God.

TRUGANINNI:
The sky dies to be born
The star lizard swims into dark
The moon's eye is not rising
We are looking with our hearts
But my father is gone
Where I dance is a dry and waterless place.

NANNA:
Where we dance is a dry and waterless place...

> *(TRUGANINNI returns to McKAY and sits beside him holding his arm)*

LEVEY: (finishing it off) And 'This is, ladies and gentlemen, is...'?

McKAY: (undertone) This is Truganinni, ladies and gentlemen.

LEVEY: And that is no fault of yours.

McKAY: It is no fault of mine.

> *(There is an extended silence, during which LEVEY and CROWTHER take their ease, and the two women step back to the kitchen's doorway.*

A job done at last, McKAY goes to the window, looks out. He double takes at what he sees, calls back over his shoulder:)

McKAY: Mr Levey, your wife…!

LEVEY: It's just the first sight, son. You'll get used to her.

McKAY: No, she just fell off the jetty and is being swept out to sea!

LEVEY: (but not moving) Damn!

McKAY: No, wait, she's being swept back in!

LEVEY: Hurrah!

McKAY: Oh Lord, she's being swept out again.

LEVEY: She's a right Indian rubber ball, that one is.

McKAY: She's being swept out again! Wait, wait. She's found…
   (*runs to the sideboard for a telescope*)
she's found a piece of drift wood!

LEVEY: She gets a grip, you wouldn't wish drift wood any worse luck.

McKAY: She's standing up on it!

LEVEY: She did all that riding bare-back in circuses, Gawdluvher.

McKAY: She's standing on it and riding a wave back to shore! She's grinning and waving and she's… walking up and down it on a wave!

34

LEVEY: Always been ahead of her time, that one has. It'll never catch on.
  (*but condescends to take up the telescope*)
'Struth, I wish she'd cover up in public.

CROWTHER: The natives are used to the old naked form, old man.
  (*then*)
May I?
  (*quickly hands telescope back*)
I see what you mean.

LEVEY: I'm sorry you had to see that, old chum. In one so young, too.

CROWTHER: No, no. I have just aged a lot.

  (There is increasing tapping on the window)

LEVEY: Don't let her in until she's been de-liced!

CROWTHER: No, old chap, I think it might be the natives acting up

LEVEY: (not his fault) Look 'ere, when I brought her along, did I claim she'd be the most calming effect they'd ever see?

  (NANNA takes charge from three white men who remain rooted to the spot in the face of possible danger).

NANNA: (calling out to them) 'Ere, you act like proper outside or don't act up at all!

  (and glares at the door until she is actually obeyed.

  Now she knows it is the time she can do what she's been wanting to do.

  She dances around laying places on the table, yet still

35

managing to take TRUGANINNI with her as she does so.

With no beg-your-pardon, she then literally hoists McKAY to the table and sits him down. Next, she drags CROWTHER to his place at the table, and then rounds up LEVEY with no less stern force. Plonks him down.

Meantime, TRUGANINNI comes from the kitchen with plates of food, and drops one in front of each man, while NANNA fetches napkins from the sideboard and tucks them into their shirts, slapping any hand away that moves to help.

Next, she inspects the scene and adjusts here and there until she is satisfied)

NANNA: Stay, stay.

(She flits back into the kitchen)

LEVEY: (to break his disbelief) I'd ask a place set for the missus if I hadn't seen her eat, ha ha.
   (*and*)
What is this, a poor man's Last Supper?

(He goes to get up and gets from the kitchen:)

NANNA: Stay!

LEVEY: Sorry, gov'nor!

(She returns with spoons, issues them and stands with arms folded)

NANNA: Eat, eat!

(McKAY and CROWTHER knows when they should obey but LEVEY stays obdurate. She points a hanging-judge's finger at him)

NANNA: Eat, eat!

LEVEY: Missus, you had your thumb in it. Do I snort or am I goin' for the port?

NANNA: 'Ere, potatoes and cod liver oil. Keep you regular. 'Ere, you want to chase after me, you lose a few pounds.

(LEVEY looks accusingly at McKAY)

McKAY: There can be mutton, but we try to think about it from the sheep's side of things.

(Before she might actually strong-arm LEVEY, she notices TRUGANINNI with the book again)

NANNA: What do you think you're on about?

TRUGANINNI: I'm reading.

NANNA: No, you're not. That's upside down, that is.

TRUGANINNI: I'm trying to read it upside down, you-so-clever.

NANNA: Dumbcluck!

(She pulls the young woman to her feet to clear the plates away. Even though the men have barely started eating, this is much to their relief. But this relief is short lived for LEVEY. NANNA is suddenly back hissing in his ear, pointing to his tea cup)

NANNA: Cmon, cmon, cmon, cmon.

LEVEY: What what what what?

(McKAY is desperately trying to help him out with tea-drinking motions)

37

LEVEY: (finally getting it) Tea.

NANNA: Milk, milk?

LEVEY: No, no.

NANNA: (getting really peeved off) Milk, milk?

NANNA: *Milk?*

LEVEY: No. No.
  (*she clicks her tongue*)
No.
  (*she clicks her tongue even more loudly*)
NO!
  (*then he sees the other two men silently pleading with him*)
Yes! Yes! Hoi, this is like hoppin' up and down on one finger.
Gawdfornicateonme.

NANNA: (clips his ear) 'Ere, none of that in here or you're
outside.

      (and storms off to the kitchen)

LEVEY: Flamin' 'ell, she could have the part of the drover's dog.

NANNA: (off) I heard that!

LEVEY: She could give exhibition bouts with my wife.

WIFE'S VOICE FROM OUTSIDE: I heard that!

      (Just then the thylacine's bark howlingly, which rises to a
      climax of animal rage or panic. This becomes all pervasive,
      to the extent that neither of the men dares to move while it's
      going on. Then its shrieks reach a peak, then a sudden
      silence.

CROWTHER: Now I admit that doesn't sound too good.

LEVEY: (but not moving) The blighters are tormentin' my tiger. Or tormentin' the missus. You'd be a piano tuner to be able to tell the diff.
   (*then to their stares*)
Orright, orright, I'm goin'…

> *(At the front door he is too late seeing the vomit and slips loudly in it. He looks at McKAY and CROWTHER in reproach, but they can only shrug. LEVEY opens the door further, tries to fight his way to get out. He is not succeeding until McKAY gets up and pushes against the crowd trying to get in. He leaves with LEVEY, slams the door behind him.*
>
> *NANNA has looked in to see what the trouble is)*

NANNA: (re vomit, overshoulder into kitchen) 'Ere, you clean this up!

TRUGANINNI: (a 'not mine' from the kitchen) It was there when I opened my eyes.

NANNA: Liar!

> *(NANNA returns to kitchen.*
>
> *There are raised voices from outside.*
>
> *CROWTHER waits at the table knowing LEVEY will be back soon. He is right. LEVEY does so, fighting his way to get in again from the crush at the door, re-takes his place at the table, is uncharacteristically silent. Finally:)*

LEVEY: They let a man's tiger out! Where's the missus with her whip when you need her?
   (*as though it's their fault*)
Don't help, will you?

CROWTHER: (declining) Surgeon's hands, old man.

LEVEY: (a stopping thought) Mind, if it gets hold of a throat or two, might be good for the publicity.
  (*'sees' sign up in lights*)
Man-eater wif No Manners! Disgusting Messes from South of the Continent! Shuddering Assured! Underfives 'Alfprice! Am I a see-er or be I a sod?

> *(The front door is opened and McKAY forces his way back in by using his elbows and a few judicious kicks)*

LEVEY: How many did it maul

McKAY: (ominously) It's not that, Mr Levey.

LEVEY: Not worse?

McKAY: I think so

LEVEY: What, man?

McKAY: They ate it. Well, they're still eating it really.

LEVEY: (yells to outside) Oi, you spit that out! That's my tiger!

McKAY: Sorry.

LEVEY: Don't you feed that lot anything?

McKAY: I can see where this is leading. It is going to land on my doorstep.

LEVEY: It's already landed on your doorstep!

> *(Suddenly the barking-howling starts up again. This time it is much nearer, maybe on the veranda itself. This doesn't matter to LEVEY, greatly relieved)*

LEVEY: Gawdluvher, that'll be the missus showing 'em nobody steals from the Leveys.

CROWTHER: A brick of a woman, I hear.

LEVEY: Any number of bricks, mark my words.
   (*mocking McKAY's assertion*)
Ate it. Ate it, me bum.

> *(The howling-barking rises again to a peak and degenerates into shrieking of human horror)*

LEVEY: Now, that don't sound right.

> *(He goes to go out again, but is abruptly stopped by NANNA.*
>
> *She looks out onto the veranda first and motions for the two men to stay where they are, before she goes out, firmly shuts the door behind her.*
>
> *Alone with his curiosity, LEVEY tries to see out through the window but can't see what is going on. He kicks his heels until NANNA returns.*
>
> *As she opens the door, we hear the crying of a newborn baby. NANNA stands back to let in TRUGANINNI who is carrying a new born child)*

LEVEY: (indicating the newborn) Lordluvher, that bread-n'-strife of mine's always been quick.

McKAY: It's not hers, silly.

> *(TRUGANINNI unceremoniously crosses to CROWTHER and puts the infant down in front of him for checking. She doesn't wait for his examination, but turns and pushes her*

41

way outside again)

CROWTHER has perfunctorily looked at the child, holds it up by the leg to NANNA, who takes it, wipes it down, clucks over it, and takes it off into the kitchen.

There is a knock on the door. McKAY moves to answer it)

LEVEY: (cowardly 'brave') If that's my missus, tell her I've got the kaks on her.

> *(McKAY listens to something said to him from the veranda, shakes his head firmly and shuts the door quickly:)*

LEVEY: (impatiently) Listen 'ere, what about my man-eatin' tiger?

McKAY: I think there's still some tail if you'd like soup.
  (*and*)
That was the mother of that child, I'm afraid.

LEVEY: Not even them what's pregnant's got a right to sink their teeth into my tiger!

McKAY: It seems it was getting all the food and attention, so the mother, she decided to… well, imitate it.

LEVEY: Don't you feed 'em here?

McKAY: (hurt) We work our fingers to the bone.

LEVEY: 'An so did my tiger!
  (*thought*)
Take that mother's name. Maybe I could use her. With that there howl of hers, throw the skin over her in a cage and who'd suss the diff, eh? And… and, how's this?, she gives birth to a human baby 'fore their very eyes! The Babe Born of Wild Beast! Never Before Attempted on Stage!' How's that?

CROWTHER
And no need to try to find another Van Diemens tiger to buy.

LEVEY: Tiger? Ha! This be theatre; who needs the real thing?
Like I always said, a penny saved is a penny you've saved; is it or
ain't it?
   (*then, rounding on McKAY*)
But the name of the newborn, like, McKie son. The billing name!

   *(McKAY is shocked at himself for forgetting, runs to
   kitchen, calls, runs back to desk)*

McKAY: The name, Nanna!
         (to others)
Always an important occasion for the Mission, don't you know.
The first in four years, alive and kicking, don't you know, ha ha.
   (*stops on thought, to CROWTHER*)
It will stay alive and kicking, do you think, Doctor?

CROWTHER: I could guess. I could get lucky.

   (McKAY pulls out his ledger)

McKAY: Mr Robinson will be delighted. He always said one day
we will be able to put a tick rather than a strike-through. We add
them up daily.

   (NANNA and TRUGANINNI come back in)

McKAY: (pen poised towards baby's crutch) What?

NANNA: A boy.

McKAY: Any distinguishing marks?

NANNA: Better'n some men I know.

McKAY: Date? Today?
   (*gets no reply*)

43

Fill that in later. Mother's name?
  (*gets no response*)
Fill that in later. Father's name?
  (*no response*)
Fill that in later
  (*brightens*)
Ah… the 'to-be-called'. Let's see… the next one should be…?
  (*has to go back right through register to find last living baby*)
Been a while since a real live one, ha ha.
  (*finds something*)
Here. … William? Any objections?
  (*writes it down*)
William. And a Lanney, methinks.
  (*triumphantly*)
My friends, we have a William Lanney within our midst!

NANNA: The Lord is great!

McKAY: Do you think you can track down the father?
  (*to their resultant sniggers*)
Well, at least try to catch the mother before she can get to her feet.
  (*to their renewed sniggers*)
Really. I do think somebody could have held her down, Nanna.

NANNA: 'Ere, I told someone to.

McKAY: Good woman! Quick, then!

        (*He jumps up and dashes hopefully outside after the
        mother, motioning NANNA and TRUGANINNI to follow.*

        *TRUGANINNI does not follow. Rather, she thrusts the
        baby into LEVEY's arms, then takes up the book again and
        gets re-absorbed in it.*

        LEVEY holds the baby up high 'for the stage lamps':)

LEVEY: Ladies, squatters and squoffers, your hands together, ta,
for our Bonny Prince William!

(*stops*)
Not quite it.
　(*tries again*)
Ladies and laughers, gents and guzzlers, let's 'ave your flippers come together for...

　　　(He raises an eyebrow to CROWTHER for suggestion)

CROWTHER: Prince, bah. His Royal Highness.

LEVEY: King Highness, right you are. King Willy.

CROWTHER: Nup.

LEVEY: (got it) Ladies and la-de-dahs, let's 'ave it for King Billy, not Willy!

CROWTHER: King Billy not Willy!

LEVEY: Billy Rex! Your right royal rectitude!
　(*looking*)
'E just peed on me. Shows he's a true man of the theatre.

　　　(But CROWTHER sees it's time to be serious. He turns to TRUGANINNI, gently takes the book from her hands)

CROWTHER: Truganinni, back to the letter I got from Reverend Robinson...

TRUGANINNI: I'm not going outside!   I'm inside!

CROWTHER: No, no. It just appears he is not coming back. The Governor has moved him on to protect you people around Port Phillip on the mainland. The real mainland.

　　　(There are collective cheers from outside. He turns to LEVEY)

CROWTHER: News travels fast around here.

(*back to her waiting silence*)
The Reverend Robinson mentions here… well, you, Truganinni. It
appears you are to be congratulated for your ten years with him.
Seems like yesterday, does it?, ha ha. I am quoting him there,
mind. As a special treat of thanks he instructs me to make sure you
get a really tripping hot bath, especially for you.

> *(She waits, knowing there is more)*

CROWTHER: Oh, and there's one thing more. Your Reverend…
not mine… has sent a gift for you. Apparently, it's two whole
bottle of your favourite gin, expense being nothing, he says, and,
to quote here: 'To be expressly taken while enjoying the really
tripping hot bath'.

TRUGANINNI: (glumly) Not again.

> *(She leaves. As a doctor, CROWTHER follows on her
> heels.*
>
> *LEVEY finally realizes he is left alone with the baby, and
> doesn't know what to do. Looking out of the window
> doesn't get him any help, nor does CROWTHER, or any
> other, return to give him company.*
>
> *He tries to settle the infant on the bed, but it threatens to
> fall off, and he has to retrieve it. Bouncing it on his knees
> doesn't help.*
>
> *He calls in an empty house:)*

.
LEVEY: Hoi? Hoiya…!
    (*nothing. Reverts to having to talk to infant*)
Wouldn't it rot your socks off, Bill? Listen 'ere, son, don't go
getting above your station and peeing where you like, ha ha. ….

> *(Finally, he gets spooked.*

*Hurries over to the front door and thrusts it wide open.
There is no one out there, not even the odd shadow of
anyone moving)*

LEVEY: HOI! HOI!

(It only echoes.

*It is obvious that he has been deliberately left alone with the
infant while the others take advantage of the rest it affords
them.*

*The baby starts crying. Terribly out of his depth, LEVEY
tries everything he can think of to silence it, then quickly
hoists him back onto the sofa)*

LEVEY: (to fill in the void) See, Bill, see? Get used to the void.
Take some advice from an old hand, son: never miss the boat. But
don't let 'em hear you howlin' too much.

(The infant stops crying as though to think about it.)

LEVEY: That's the ticket. You just think what they can throw at
yer if you go on howlin' too much, laddie.
   (*and*)
You want old uncle Barnett, just start howlin'. I'll be outside.

(LEVEY moves towards leaving.

*The baby falls from the sofa onto the floor with a loud
thump, which brings LEVEY hurrying back.*

*He stands looking down at it expectantly, but is relieved to
see it is all right, quickly picks it up and deposits it back on
the sofa, this time secured and safely)*

LEVEY: Gawdluvyer, a true troubadour, bouncing back like that.
Havin' a thick skull won't hurt yer with a lot of thick heads you'll

47

get later, let me tell you, King Bill. An' don't forget what I told you about that boat, son. Alrightee then, see you in the soup, eh?

(He leaves)

(end Act 1)

Act 2
King Billy's Going

(A darkened stage. Gradually theatrical lamp lighting comes up in the foreground (only).

It is the stage of the old Royal Theatre and it is 1877, a whole year after the death of Truganinni.

The only initial props are at the very front of the stage -- at one side, a fire-side chair and, at the other, an early wheelchair.

BARNETT LEVEY – now an old man – comes on stage to address the audience. He stands centre stage and is obviously well used to facing an auditorium of people alone and centralized. He is dressed just as gaudily (in style of an old London busker) as he was in the first Act.

He waves to the audience to stay a little more patient, clears his throat, then breaks out, howbeit so shakily given his age, into a song which he has become known for over the years to start all of the theatre he has ever put on...)

LEVEY:
　　In Dublin's fair city,
　　Where the girls are so pretty,
　　I first set my eyes on sweet Molly Malone,
　　As she wheeled her wheel-barrow,
　　Through streets broad and narrow
　　Crying "Cockles and mussels, alive, alive, oh!"
　　Alive, alive, oh,
　　Alive, alive, oh!
　　Crying "Cockles and mussels, alive, alive, oh"…

　　(He has to stop to croak a bit. Then reverts to speech:)

49

LEVEY: Gawd, I missed usin' the old vocals. Yes, cock-o's, I am still in the land of the living. If I am a ghost, how come th'missus keeps complaining of my fluffin'? If you see me go past, don't worry, it's me; who's ever seen a ghost chasing its own tail. Ha ha. I tell yer what, though… Gawd, I miss serenading you lot nightly!

(*then*)

Oi, that there new management says I'm too old n' 'ad it to serenade you anymore. Well, did I have the tears running down your eyes just then or what? Either that or you lot're in the trenches without any ammo left.

(*also*)

No, we're 'ere to be serious, so you lot up in the Gods get your hands orf each other. We're 'ere tonight, ladles and gentmen, to commemorate it bein' ten old years, plus, since old King Billy kakked it. Why, wasn't I, the first bloke to cradle him in these very arms down in old Van Diemens Land. I cradles him; he cradled me; we did it for warmth down in that place, ha ha.

(*and*)

Okay, okay. But you've been special invited 'ere tonight to doff yer caps and tip yer hats on the now-a-whole-year's-flamin'-gone-by anniversary of the passing of his queen… well, we all wanted 'er to be, didn't we?... his fellow Tasso-the-manian in bein' able to hang in there… drum roll please, maestro…

(He gets one and gets lighting on the empty wheelchair)

LEVEY: Enuff of that.

(*carries on rhetoric*)

Yes, King Bill's Tasso-in-manian ultimate surrrr-vivor, Queen Truganinni! Put yer two-by-fives together!...

(*drum roll again and emphasis on emptiness of wheelchair*)

Cos the Queen can't be 'ere on account of dying a year ago. But that's what we're 'ere for, right?

(provokes confirming catcalls, clapping etc)

Gawdluvher, I woulda cradled her too in them days for a bit o' warmth but I couldn't catch her between…

(*makes belly pregnant motions for laughs*)

50

belly wind. Know what I mean?
  (*but seriously*)
Gawdluvher.

  (*He goes over to the fire-side chair, sits, pulls out a cigar
  and lights it, crosses legs and settles back*)

LEVEY: So I'm just going to settle down 'ere, like I'm sitting on
'er lap… an' no mistakin' any smile what comes to me face, you
dirty-minded lot you, while Barnett Levey & Sons presents for
your delections its last tribute to old queenly Truganinni and King
Bill and the whole blessed lot o' them. I'd 'ave done it m'self but
me old knees are shakier than my sons is at stage writin', ha ha…
  (*and 'presenting'*)
It's called 'Act 2: King Billy's Going'.

  (*Behind him, lighting comes up on CROWTHER's doctor's
  room, Hobart town, 1869.*

  *It is almost a replica of the room at the Mission house of
  Act 1, except it has urbanised finery.*

  At the centre is King Billy's coffin.

  *It is funeral day. The table, and the floor beneath the coffin
  are strewn with flowers.*

  For a long moment this coffin is the centre of focus.

  *Finally, NANNA… reflecting being older by 40 or so years,
  as others from Act 1 will… enters. She unceremoniously
  clatters around CROWTHER's desk, showing scant regard
  for his work, uses feather duster and her fingers to get the
  dust and dead bugs off.*

  *TRUGANINNI has wandered lassitudinously in behind her.
  She has gone over to the coffin and lain her head on it. By
  her sad yet still-at-work manner, she has already done
  much of her grieving over her male counterpart – or at least*

51

as much as CROWTHER has allowed.

NANNA is certainly not against her sorrow… she is grieving herself… but is just more job-at-hand on this public-arriving day:)

NANNA: Here, a little help, you!

TRUGANINNI: (not lifting her head) Old woman.

NANNA: Out back and put 'em up, you call me old woman again!
  (*and*)
Push them chairs over by the wall.

TRUGANINNI: Why would I want to push the chairs over?

NANNA: Push them out of the way. Don't keep arguing.

TRUGANINNI: How can people sit in the way if I push them over there out of the way.

NANNA: (disgusted) That's it. After today, you're outside!

(TRUGANINNI has obviously learnt over the years to ignore threats like that. Besides, CROWTHER has heard their exchange as he enters)

CROWTHER: Ladies, ladies. Today of all days, let's try to be a bit solemn.

NANNA: What's Sodom?

CROWTHER: Solemn.

NANNA: (mumble) Solemn and Gomorrah, what'll they think of next?

(NANNA strains to pick up the flowers from the floor)

52

CROWTHER: Actually, I left them down there deliberately, Nanna. I like the Hindu temple look, don't you?

NANNA: (ominously) Something wrong about today.

CROWTHER: Don't you be worrying about that.

(He is trying to find something at his desk, but NANNA has really disarranged it)

CROWTHER: (with half a mind) Don't let me stop anyone from walking the dog.

NANNA: (at TRUGANINNI) Haven't you walked the dog?

TRUGANINNI: You walk the dog.
  (pointing to her 'below')
I'm oozing.

NANNA: You're always oozing. What about my oozing?

TRUGANINNI: Who wants to go near you when you're oozing?

NANNA: As far as I'm concerned, that's outside talk, that is.

TRUGANINNI: You should be glad the dog wouldn't care.

CROWTHER: Truganinni, you go powder yourself. Everybody will be looking at you today.

TRUGANINNI: (just plain truculent) I've got to walk the dog yet.

CROWTHER: Please, go.

NANNA: You heard the master.

(TRUGANINNI leaves with a spring in her step)

53

CROWTHER: Anyone arrived yet, Nanna?

NANNA: Not last time I looked, sir.

CROWTHER: Don't refuse entrance to anybody, understand? Everybody's welcomed. The invitations went out?

NANNA: They did, sir. Shall I leave the door open, then?

CROWTHER: Best. Nobody might come, but then the whole town might turn out.

> *(He turns to her, surprisingly engaged by a thought. Indicates the coffin:)*

CROWTHER: Nanna, poor old Billy here… I've been meaning to ask you… You know, there was a time when I thought she and… King Billy… well, the age difference, I suppose. Older woman and all that, but only by a few years…

NANNA: (with surprising great pride) M'Tru's very particular, sir. And…
   (indicates coffin)
Bill, he was a bit obstinate, sir.

CROWTHER: I know. But, still, last chances for the people, and all that. You would have thought they'd give it a bit of a go. Him known as King; she as his Queen. Neat that way.

NANNA: My Tru said he was always oozing too much for her. She's even more particular about oozing on street corners like he did.

CROWTHER: Pity. As I said, last chance and all that. Not recently, mind. But there was a time earlier, don't you think? But still we're all passed by time.

NANNA: Oozing.

CROWTHER: The oozes. Yes, I suppose you're right.

NANNA: (defendingly) 'Ere, my Tru'd still give any man a go, sir.

CROWTHER: As you say, Nanna, as you say. I'll take your word. Spilt milk, I suppose.
  (*pause*)
Speaking of spilt milk, I hear that our illustrious Governor is coming. Rumour has it he's one of the few of our age still on the udder.

> *(There is a long pause. She waits for more instructions. He is engrossed by thoughts of public opinion)*

CROWTHER: You know, Nanna, I intend to bury him properly, don't you?

NANNA: I don't know anything, Dr.

CROWTHER: ('coming back') Sorry. I meant them out there. Hobart. They think I'm going *to do something* to him. Do you know why they might be thinking that?

NANNA: (getting alarmed) I don't know about that.

CROWTHER: (hotly) I only took him from the Government mortuary this morning to…

> *(looks at her blank face, gives up)*

NANNA: You'll have your reasons, sir.

CROWTHER: So you heard that?

NANNA: This is Hobart town, sir.

CROWTHER: (sudden and desperate) He was the last one. Don't you see what that means… the need to allow him to keep a duty towards the world's knowledge for generations to come?

NANNA: (very warily) Truganinni's the last one now, Doctor.

CROWTHER: (getting himself in a knot) And by God that's why she's in this house, preserved. Protected. Preserved and protected.
  (then)
Something told me to intervene this morning, and I stand by it.

NANNA: Good, sir. It's a lovely lot of flowers.

CROWTHER: The government would have just thrown him in a hole some secret place and shoveled him over. That Governor and his anti-the-scientific-community... it's all around us, keeping us on guard.
  (then)
At least now there'll be guests.
  (getting up steam)
By God, full rites and the full six feet in the bottle. There mightn't be any left to throw a spear into the air, but we can give Billy to the future!
  (swings on her, looking desperate for comfort)
Nanna, I ask you, the whole future or peace in the ground?

NANNA: (alarmed again) A piece of what, Dr Crowther?

CROWTHER: Never mind.

NANNA: Haven't we got a piece of ground for the lad, Doctor?

CROWTHER: Yes, yes, of course we have. All I was asking was what's so undebatable about dust to dust? Aren't we all…
  (heavily)
pickled in the same jar?

(NANNA points to the specimens he has on his shelves)

56

NANNA: (now very suspicious) You wouldn't be meaning like these, would you, sir?

CROWTHER: (laughs) Like my College of Surgeons way off in London? Oh, you're sharp for a woman of your age, Nanna. I've heard those rumours too.
  (*and*)
Do you remember by chance all those years ago and that theatre chap from Sydney coming over to the island and wanting to buy what he called the theatrical rights?

NANNA: Yes.

CROWTHER: Well, something like that.
  (*then*)
Bless me, I don't know why we're talking about all this. Let's just say King Billy, the last man, is going to rest in my house for a while. Now, let's get back to business, shall we?

> *(She waits for what he means by 'business', but he has turned away to be engrossed in writing something at his desk. She waits as long as patience allows, then goes to move out)*

CROWTHER: I'd prefer you to stay, Nanna.

> *(and he simply gets up to leave her alone with the coffin.*
>
> *But as he is leaving, he has to make room for MOLLY, the bar maid, to come boldly in. True to his reputation, he swings around from leaving and follows her back in.*
>
> *She walks around the coffin dabbing her eyes, then takes a seat)*

CROWTHER: You belong around here, Miss?

MOLLY: Where this type of laying around the place goes on? Not on your nellie, if that's what you mean.

NANNA: Here, you mind your pardon.

MOLLY: I haven't got one, girl. It's a lovely day outside. I got to talking with a spotted dog. Old Billy would have loved it out today. Out of the box, this day is, not meaning Billy here, ha ha. The Dog and Patridge's where I serve. So should I be here? I should not, but I came for Bill's sake, I did.
   (*she goes over to the coffin*)
Bill? I've seen you better, lovey.
   (*remembers*)
Wait, wait.

> *(She produces a shilling, and ceremoniously places on the coffin)*

NANNA: 'Ere, I just varnished that.

MOLLY: G'arn, let him have it. He gave me enough of them, truth be known. Billy? It's Molly, love. It's all right.

> *(They momentarily have nothing more to say to each other, finally sit and either side of the room. They wait, MOLLY deliberately avoiding CROWTHER's glad eye)*

CROWTHER: So welcome, then, Miss Molly.

MOLLY: You the owner?

CROWTHER: I am.

MOLLY: (looking about) Not bad. Bill wouldn't be objecting.

NANNA: 'Ere, it's no good you getting fresh.

CROWTHER: It's all right, Nanna.
   (to MOLLY)

You're our first, Miss.

MOLLY: Better'n lingering around the streets talking to spotted dogs.
   (*and*)
See, what I think is he queered his luck last weekend. Some reason, Billy gives me a few coin on account. Never mind on what account. I'm not kidding. On the tab, like. Bad luck to do that. Get it in but don't give it out beforehand, is what anyone'd say, right? But even spotting them whales like he did, they'd all say, what a tryer. He might have been black, but he was a bit of an Abo. You can tell by their eyes when they can't leave it alone.
   (*then pause*)
Them blessed street brats were the worse. They'd be throwing rocks at him and him strolling along mindin' his own business. 'Darkie, give's a dance'. What a thing to say. I'd be telling him, 'Don't you be taking any mind, Bill'.
   (*pause*)
Off he'd come from that ship and into the Dog and Partridge. I said to him, I said, go home to your people, lovey. Git. No way, he says. 'Them's all old ladies with no teeth with their old hands always trying to swing me anchor.' And the likes o' this...
   (*indicates around, meaning CROWTHER by implication*)
telling him not to pay for it, give it to one of those old ladies for free. No way, he says again. 'What sort of kid'd come out of one of those?' 'Apart from the teeth whatnot,' I said, 'what's wrong with that? They're you own kind, isn't it?' 'I want me boy to be able to walk down the street', he said. 'What?', I says, 'sporting a face like yours?' Good old laugh we had with that one.
   (*pause*)
And you talk about famous. Bill was famous.

CROWTHER: (with own meaning) Well... Not quite. Not alive.

MOLLY: (not picking up on that) He met Prince Alfred that time. Prince Alfred, none of your down-the-line trash. Cakes and tea on that royal yacht big as a royal's palace itself. La-de-dah and there's Billy spilling the bubbly all over himself like he just wet

59

himself. The Prince going haw haw. My Billy boy going bloody hell, where's the swab? It's a real shame he's here.
(*dabs her eyes*)
That's his shilling really. I wish I could 'ave paid it on account, like he did.
(*finally does turn to CROWTHER*)
Who's going to do you when your time's come?

CROWTHER: Oh, I'm a doctor. I know it all off by heart!

> *(He realizes he has said something foolish, turns away in self-retribution.*
>
> *To NANNA's distaste, MOLLY has made herself at home by now. She gets up and walks around the coffin inspecting it, rubbing off any marks she sees)*

NANNA: 'Ere, any dirty mark's mine!

MOLLY: Wouldn't be the first time one of you gals has said that about old Bill.

NANNA: 'Ere, you, what 'you gals'?

MOLLY: (just shrugging) 'Let 'em dream on, Bill', I used to tell him.

NANNA: (ready to attack) 'Ere, I'm inside, not outside! You ever seen me outside?

> *(CROWTHER has been patient up until now. He sees he'd better intervene. He makes a painter's gesture of seeing MOLLY framed on canvas against the light, and:)*

CROWTHER: A vision. Stay exactly where you are.

MOLLY: No hope, that. I've come to be respectable, not talk to gentlemen. But I tell you what…
(*beckons him to the coffin with her*)

MOLLY: Come and catch a look.
  (*to NANNA*)
You, too. For our Billy, just a peep. He won't bite, you know.
Hardly a tooth left, young as he was. I lost them sinking them into
whales, he said. A real kidder, wasn't he ever.

  (They stand solemnly looking down at the coffin)

CROWTHER: I bought him into the world, don't you know.
Well, I almost got there in time to bring him into the world. But I
cut the cord. If I remember it was difficult to get out of bed those
days. Flinders Island. Cold. Hard to get a hold on that cord to
cut.

MOLLY: Them street brats and their rocks. 'Darkie, give's a
dance.' Right charming, and the State paying for their schoolin'.

  *(They wait for NANNA to add her bit, but she can think of
  nothing to say. Finally:)*

CROWTHER: (still musing) It could have been an anchor rope,
the way he sailed on.

MOLLY: What?

CROWTHER: The cord.

MOLLY: If they'd seen old Bill like I seen old Bill, they'd put
them brats on a whaler and old Bill into school. What he should
have done was cut 'em. I don't mean chopped 'em. I mean make
the brats laugh. Billy could do that with one of his jigs-o. That
sort of cutting.

CROWTHER: (before biting his lip) Or use a scalpel.

MOLLY: (shudders) I 'ate talk of scalpels.

CROWTHER: (forces himself back into urbanity) It's just a word, Miss Molly. Scalpels. An incisive word.
(*now very comfortable again settled back at desk*)
A sharp and right-to-the-quick word. It's a word that adds spice to splice. Scalpel, scalped. You see, the thing is, Miss, I do not hide from being a scalpelist, and never have. It's all to do with what kind of result you are aiming for. A good dressing or a bad dressing, in which case you'd get a good dressing-down, ha ha.

> *(The woman are shocked by his feeble humour and loud laugh.*
>
> *He stops abruptly. Long pause. MOLLY returns to a seat. NANNA hears something outside the room, goes out to take a look.*
>
> *Eventually, in the following 'emptiness', NANNA steps back to let COLVIN, the part-time whaling-boat captain and part-time undertaker, come in.*
>
> *COLVIN has his cap in hand, but that is about all that is respectful in his manner, which is a strange mixture of courteousness and aggression for such an occasion.*
>
> *He nods curtly to CROWTHER, does a reverent round of the coffin as MOLLY did.*
>
> *As he does so, NANNA takes the opportunity to confidentially inform CROWTHER:)*

NANNA: The undertaker, sir.

CROWTHER: A sailor too?

> *(she nods, and whispers:)*

NANNA: Colvin, sir.

CROWTHER: (whispered back) The coalman too?

NANNA: (long suffering) The name. Dr. Colvin.

CROWTHER: (the welcoming host) Ah, Mr Colvin…

COLVIN: Captain.

CROWTHER: (corrected) Ah, Captain Colvin, our undertaker!

COLVIN: If it's the undertaker, then it's Mr.

CROWTHER: Mister. And very good!

COLVIN: (accusatorily) You took my coffin away from the Government stores where I had it.

CROWTHER: I did, yes. Properly requisitioned.

COLVIN: That right?

CROWTHER: It is, indeed.

COLVIN: Come to see if it's stood up.

CROWTHER: No, it's been laid flat like that all the time, I assure you.

(COLVIN just stares at him as though he was a simpleton)

CROWTHER: Oh, 'stood up'. It's stood up okay. No bouncing around, I assure you.

COLVIN: And to ask why since that coffin belongs to me and m'ship mates.

CROWTHER: Really? Not the Government's?

COLVIN: They ain't paid for it yet.

CROWTHER: Sorry, sorry. But you see it's in good hands now.

COLVIN: All I see is Bill being mucked around with.

CROWTHER: If you believe in the Grand Design, Mister Colvin…

COLVIN: Captain, if it's not the undertaker you're addressing, like I said.

CROWTHER: Maybe you did. But if you do believe in the Grand Design, you'd know we're only all servants of the greater good. We've all got to go and end up in someone else's hands, not our mother's, no?

COLVIN: A good-enough life's been taken today. I gave Bill my best hands, if you're on about that. Did you?

CROWTHER: I did and have.
   (*back in his comfort zone*)
You know, Captain or Mister, I've come to think life's all a bit sticky, don't you think?

COLVIN: I don't know nothing about that. I've only come to…

CROWTHER: No, wait. I mean sticky as in, we buzz and then we get stuck in that fly paper they're selling now. You take this room, this coffin. You take these flowers. You take me…

COLVIN: You'll be taken one day.

CROWTHER: And you, sir.

COLVIN: Not by you.

CROWTHER: By all of us in a sense, sir. All waiting for the unerring sticky end. In your sailing parlance, he's just there, stowed away his bones waiting for all of us to stow ours.
   (*then craftily*)

It's just where our bones get stowed, you see. Might as well be somewhere in particular, I think you'll agree.

COLVIN: It's jokin' time now, is it?

(He goes to the coffin, inspects it very closely)

COLVIN: (diversionary) Billy was one of your crew?
  (*knowing the answer*)
I hear whaling's been hard for years.

COLVIN: Where's the Government in all of this?

MOLLY: (piping up) Where it always is. Probably snoozin' in there alongside of our Bill.

(COLVIN looks scathingly at her)

COLVIN: Yes, I've heard about you.

MOLLY: Then you are either naughty or nice.

COLVIN: (*back to CROWTHER*) Is this a blasted funeral or what?

CROWTHER: Bring your men in, Captain… respectfully, mind… and then maybe we can start.

COLVIN: There's just one thing me and the lads want to know before we join up. I heard you hedge a lot. You're going to hedge around one simple question?

CROWTHER: Ask it.

COLVIN: Why'd you stop the government doing it all nice'n'quiet last night?

CROWTHER: King Billy deserved more.

COLVIN: (hotly) Who're you to say so? Now, we'll break our backs carrying him, but only if it's not a sham.

CROWTHER: That sounds threatening.

COLVIN: (the condition) We've heard something about Bill being tampered with. So, matey, I'm opening this box.

CROWTHER: Not in this house, you won't be!

> *(This keys on a dangerous confrontation between them.*
>
> *Unnoticed, NANNA had left the room and now returns with some information to whisper to CROWTHER. It breaks the confrontation)*

CROWTHER: It seems the Colonial Secretary is here.

> *(In his fireside chair, at centre left, LEVEY starts, although, with age, he takes a time to get to his feet. While he struggles to, he speaks to the audience.*
>
> *NOTE: LEVEY continues to speak to the audience while he acts the part of ATWELL the Colonial Secretary even though he's supposed to be part of the play. Nor does he bother to join the others in the 'play area'; he just stays close to his fireside chair:)*

LEVEY: Oi, somebody say 'Colonial Secretary'? That's me! Why's it me you might ask? Cos the budget don't run into another greedy actor mouth to feed, so me sons tell me, an' at my age I come the cheapest in the family, right?
   (over his shoulder to the acting area)
Say again, son.

CROWTHER: It seems the Colonial Secretary is here.

LEVEY AS ATWELL: Hold yer 'orses there a bit, Doccco.
   (clears throat and 'acts' the government official)

66

Now, Captain Colvin, careful with those hands of yours. One day you're going to drop in them yourself

COLVIN: You, I don't know.

CROWTHER: Giles Atwell from the Government.

LEVEY AS ATWELL: I was in the neighbourhood, William.

CROWTHER: You're never just in the neighbourhood, Giles.

LEVEY AS ATWELL: That's not true, of course.

CROWTHER: Not when you're needed.

LEVEY AS ATWELL: That's true too.
  (*obviously to COLVIN*)
Returning to what you were saying, Captain. My advice would be to let the box stay as it is.

CROWTHER: (quickly answers instead) The Governor sent you, Mr Atwell?

LEVEY AS ATWELL: Does it matter if he did, William?

CROWTHER: Who's ever stopped you?

LEVEY AS ATWELL: Sometimes they do, William, I'm always glad to be among people with the same interests as myself, though. 'Interests' here would imply 'amusements', I dare say.

COLVIN: You find this amusing?
  (*and, indicating coffin*)
You let him snitch this from under your nose.

LEVEY AS ATWELL: No, sir, we are fairly fine with it. A bit more finery while laying in the ground and all that.

COLVIN: But you being here… you sayin' the Government did or didn't give permission for this?

LEVEY AS ATWELL: One way or another, probably yes, Captain. We'd just like a little peek in there too, if that's all right, William?

MOLLY: Here, it that allowed? I mean, would you like it?

LEVEY AS ATWELL: Hello, Molly.

MOLLY: Hello, Coochie. How's the rash?

LEVEY AS ATWELL: Like this 'ere coffin, dear lady, it's just a question of property not propriety. Isn't that right, William?

(CROWTHER doesn't answer. COLVIN, needing no extra excuses, is already working at opening the coffin)

MOLLY: That's my shilling I just gave Bill up there.

(They wait while COLVIN gets the lid off.

He reels back at what he sees. Even CROWTHER has to come forward to take a look…)

COLVIN: (recovers first) Which of you butchers deserves to have his throat cut first?

(LEVEY 'drops' his ATWELL characterization, confides to audience 'outside' of play:)

LEVEY: Luvvers and luggers, because me cigar's goin' out, I'll cut to the chase. It was like when the Government heard them Royal College of Surgeons were gonna have at Billy's earthly remains, like, they jumped in first. Like just our taxes, eh?, ha ha. Anyways, they lop of old Bill's hands'n'feet so old Crowther can't send his pals in London town what's anything worth havin'. But before they get round to buryin' him, the lazy sods, along comes

68

Crowther, so the diddly-erd goes, and he gets all peeved at not
havin' a healthy skelo. So he ups'n'slits Billy's head an' whips
out his skull replacin' it with the skull of some poor white codger
what died in the hospital that night.

 (*and*)

Who'd be the white codger for starters, right?

 (*and*)

So then everybody's 'appy-'appy. The Guv's 'appy the Surgeons
ain't got all a' Bill and the Surgeons're 'appy the Guvment's ain't
got the whole thing neither. While our King Billy's lying' there
without skull, hands nor feet and Gawd knows what else. Now, 'e
ain't too 'appy, bet London to a brick on it. Am I right or am I a
regular?

> *(He directs audience back to 'play area')*

COLVIN: (to CROWTHER) Why'd you have to do that?

> *(CROWTHER turns away admitting nothing. LEVEY*
> *resumes his ATWELL part as he re-puffs on his cigar)*

LEVEY AS ATWELL: Suppose you're going to ask me next.
Why? I don't think I fully know myself.

 (*delighted to trouble-make*)

Doctor William Crowther of the Royal College of Surgeons, do
you have any idea of the whys?

 (*gets only a vitriolic look in return*)

I take it that's an invitational decline.

> *(In the resulting hiatus…)*

COLVIN: He was as good a man as you'd get. As strong an'
willing as any I ever walked the deck with, an' that's a fact. He'd
have bred all right if you'd have kept a few of their lasses up to it.
We had one of them photographs taken of the crew a while back.
Our Bill, he didn't like it. He was too 'black' for him, he said.
Too 'black'. We had him thinking like that, and that was a blessed
shame.

69

LEVEY AS ATWELL: All I might say is: we huff and we puff in this world, but one or two of us do so watched. King Billy was one. What I can concede is he belonged to the wider world, but no one should take any credit for that. I don't think we know where he really came from, what his people were, what his real name was, but from the minute he got carried inside, all Billy's life was a public performance. The only thing wrong about all that is I could be wrong or I could be right.

COLVIN: He was our good mate at sea, the top-of-the-mast man. They don't come often, not as good as he was. Eyes sharp as they come when it came to horizons.

MOLLY: He didn't owe anything. He always paid up. Sometimes on account, would you believe.

COLVIN: I can say this. At sea, him being black didn't worry us as much as it did him.

MOLLY: I'll never forget those street brats and their stones. Darkie. Dance. What a thing.

COLVIN: You'd see old black women, slack as a whale's belly, poking and pinching him as he passed. Him asking every one of them how's their lower yardarm swingin', up to it?, even that one I knows living here?

NANNA: (piping up angrily at last) 'Ere, that's my Tru you're talking about. And me!

COLVIN: That's the one. He weren't trying to be smart. It was a sort of duty he felt, you'd suppose.
    (pointing at NANNA)
Them cacklin' back at him. And he'd tell us things, riding out quiet nights, no whales. One I keep remembering. A boy, and his mother putting a lizard in his hand and humming:
Be good
Be kind
Do not steal

Do not touch things that belong to others
Do not touch any such thing
Be good
Be kind
  (*then*)
Things like that get you.

> *(LEVEY does a little Irish gig as best he can at his age, and pronounces very inappropriately:*

LEVEY AS ATWELL: Well, off we go then!

COLVIN: Aye.

> *(He goes to shut up the coffin, but doesn't even get the lid nearly on when TRUGANINNI pushes past a restraining NANNA and walks up to the open coffin.*
>
> *When she sees what is inside, she screams and faints.*
>
> *NANNA rushes to her. Her and MOLLY help her out)*

CROWTHER: For God's sake, just put the lid back on and let's take him!

> *(COLVIN does so and calls for pall-bearing assistance as he does so:)*

COLVIN: Lads, get in here!

> *(Blackout on 'play area'*
>
> *LEVEY is left alone front stage. He settles back into his fireside chair)*

LEVEY: An' that, Gawdluvyerall, is King Billy gone. But don't go trying to follow the coffin through them streets of Hobart town and leavin'. We've still got lots more and you're goin' to 'ate it if you go and find out later I come into me own after the int'mission.

(*puffs and*)
No, straight up, I do. If the eldest of mine weren't so mean, we'd
'ave show boards hangin' up around the place saying th'next part
goes: 'Act 3 or Billyboy Gone: Where Barnett Levey Returns To
The Stage Starring In The Queen Truganinni Saga! Not To Be
Missed! Bar Sales Discounted!'

(blackout)

(End Act 2)

Act 3
Billyboy Gone

(Lighting on a room in Hobart town that, as a Victorian one, resembles the sets of the earlier Acts, distinguished by a French window opening out onto the front garden.

The room has a bright and leafy aspect.

It is where ALEXANDER McKAY has lodged TRUGANINNI (with NANNA) to convalesce.

LEVEY's fireside chair and the wheelchair have gone from the front-stage wings.

TRUGANINNI sits on a wheel chair, her legs covered with a blanket. On either side of her are two tables, on which there are the appurtenances of someone being ill for some time.

NANNA is, as always, hovering 'by' her.

They remain in frieze, as BARNETT LEVEY comes on stage in a grand entrance, which, of course, he orchestrates by playing the audience)

LEVEY: Brrrr. Brrrr. Brrrr. Brrr-rrrr, I say. This 'ere Hobart town. To my mind, no wonder they laid the foundation stone on a pile of fire n' brimstone an' then wonder why their church doors don't open. The way I'm shaking, th'missus must 'ave followed me down from Sydney.
  (then)
You ask what am I doin' 'ere? You didn't? Well, you should've 'ave! Down 'ere on a matter of a fur seal or two an' I thought to m'self I'll pop in to old Alexander Robert McKay's ne'er-to-roam once I hear old Truganinni's not takin' Billy's come-to-it too

73

kindly. It's a big 'ouse an' old Maccie's become a bit o' a right toff o'er the years, right enough, so the old gal's got all she wants late in life.

(*pause*)

So all you lot sittin' comfy? 'Ere goes…

> (*He turns and joins McKAY to enter together into TRUGANINNI's room, and they do so with care. LEVEY moves to look into TRUGANINNI's eyes, gets not much of a response, pats her on the head… goes to do the same to NANNA and gets the brush-off… turns to McKAY)*

LEVEY: So, Alex-the-phallics, how bad is it?

McKAY: You remember William Crowther?

LEVEY: Never did swing 'is theatrical rights. Still dances up a bit of a storm?

McKAY: William's a good doctor, but he just can't find anything wrong with her.

LEVEY: Not even with her wheezin'? I remember right I nearly bought him out cos of his handlin' the wheezin'. Deft 'and, that one 'ad.

McKAY: I said to him there must be something. With Billy, there was nothing obvious, either, but at least there was at least diarrhea.

LEVEY: There's diarrhea 'ere?

CROWTHER: I think so.

LEVEY: You smell so?

CROWTHER: I think so.

LEVEY: Well, that's a bit of a relief anyway, ha ha.

74

McKAY: She's refusing most of the food now.

LEVEY: Don't sound too good.

McKAY: She never recovered from what happened to Billy, of course.

LEVEY: Wouldn't be healthy if she did.

McKAY: That's true.

LEVEY: Am I right or just rigid from the cold?

(McKAY goes over and bends close to TRUGANINNI to look into her dull eyes)

McKAY: Your old friend, Mr Levey, has come to see you, Truganinni.

(There is no response from her. He turns to NANNA)

McKAY: You tell her, Nanna.

(NANNA shrugs. It is clear to all, other than McKAY she has no interest in do so)

LEVEY: 'Ere, remember when she fainted, that day of the coffin?

McKAY: I wasn't there.

LEVEY: That right? Memory's goin' as fast as I've got the runs. Me at one end o' her; that government bloke and that there sea captain on the other, but the only thing that lifted was her skirt. As if old Billy weren't a terrible sight as it was, ha ha.

McKAY: I used to send her out for a bit of fresh air. How could I know so many would stop and start poking at her like some kind of curiosity. Which she probably is.

75

LEVEY: Aye.

McKAY: Mind you, I don't take any blame for that. It's just that by the time she got back here she was even more of a wreck. It was only for fresh air, for God's sake.

LEVEY: Wot she's seen, who can blame her for wanting to act the tragedienne. Not so sick, I could use her up at the Royal. Pinch her cheeks, get a bit o' colour up.

> *(Together they look sadly over at TRUGANINNI. They do so for so sagely long that NANNA edges herself to stand between them and her friend)*

LEVEY: Wot you've taken on, Alex son, is a heavy weight.

McKAY: I consider it my duty.
  (*then telltale fierce whisper*)
But I wouldn't want her to be seen passing on here.

LEVEY: That right? Looks to me, maybe you'd better start moving on a bit quick, then.

McKAY: I'd hope I might buck her up if I take down her story.

LEVEY: That's the ticket. Do you both good. Let's 'ave a look at it when you're finished. Might be something in it for at least a matinee back at the Royal.

McKAY: Trouble is I don't know how to start.

LEVEY: Start at the beginning, lad. Across the horizon come these strange ships with sails on 'em and no shaking the spears can make 'em go away…

McKAY: No, *how* to start. Not since the doctor says he can't do anything with her.

LEVEY: Oh well, you've got your work cut out there, then.
  (*then seriously for him*)
That Society of Surgeons lot been in touch?

McKAY: You'd have to ask Dr Crowther, but I'd be a bit
surprised if they hadn't.

LEVEY: Bit o' a bunch of ghouls, if I ain't a red man with me
war paint on. Now, them, I could use up at the Royal.

McKAY: Well, they did miss out on exhibiting…
  (*so TRUGANINNI doesn't hear*)
you-know-who. They're not the types to miss out on the next.

LEVEY: I'll bet you're right there.
  (*looking at her, then earnestly to the other man*)
Look, old son, you can call me Ernest if you like, but I'll be frank
with you. With that story of hers, I wouldn't take too long 'bout
it.

  (*In the ensuing pause, McKAY endeavours to get sunny:*)

McKAY: (to NANNA) Will she try to walk today, Nanna? We
don't want her legs to get useless.

NANNA: (but kindly) She always been useless.

McKAY: Now that our old friend Mr Levey is here… we can all
sit around and think how it's been a long time since Flinders
Island, hasn't it, Nanna?

NANNA: Here, I'm still a Spring chicken. An' Tru here's no
wish bone!

McKAY: No, of course not.
  (*covers up his awkwardness by addressing LEVEY*)
Well, I'll let you three get re-acquainted. I'll just go and tell the
kitchen you'll be staying, but it might take a while.

LEVEY: (a bit alarmed) Just tell 'em and pop back.

McKAY: No, *I* am the kitchen and if I'm not careful you know what chaos kitchens and I can get into.

> *(He leaves the room.*
>
> *Left alone the women totally ignore him – so totally, in fact, that he 'goes back' to just being a narrator.*
>
> *Very soon after they have ascertained McKAY has really left, TRUGANINNI and NANNA become full of life. They start giggling and poking each other, then settle back into doing some word puzzle of the day, quite ignorant of LEVEY)*

LEVEY: (to audience) The good thing was, luggers and gaderene, that yours truly was such a good friend they treated me like I didn't even exist. Am I a vision or a vision of loveliness?...
  (*then pointing out what the woman are doing*)
'Ave to laugh, but as soon as old Macca left, and like you could see through me, they start pulling out this board game n' carryin' on…

> *(They start up again on whatever picture or word puzzle they quickly had hidden when McKAY and LEVEY arrived)*

TRUGANINNI: (impatiently) Well?

NANNA: What, well?

TRUGANINNI: What's the time lag?

NANNA: Time lag? How many letters?

TRUGANINNI: Dopey.

NANNA: Hey!

TRUGANINNI: 'How many letters'. It's a picture puzzle!

NANNA: So?

TRUGANINNI: (long-sufferingly tries again) What's the oldest word in the English language?

NANNA: In pictures?

TRUGANINNI: (eyes upwards, long suffering) What's the oldest word in the English language.

(NANNA thinks hard and desperately. Has brainwave…)

NANNA: Oldest?
  (*then inspiration*)
'Grandmother'!

TRUGANINNI: What?

NANNA: (quickly corrects) 'Grandfather'!

TRUGANINNI: What?

NANNA: 'Greatgrandmother'! 'Greatgrandfather'!

TRUGANINNI: Dumbcluck!

NANNA: 'Greatgreatgrandmother! Greatgreatgrandfather!

TRUGANINNI: (*exasperation)* Droopy-drawers!

NANNA: Hey! Who're you calling droopy?

TRUGANINNI: Droopy!

(She tosses the board off her lap, wheels her chair around and then takes off doing the rounds of the room in what is evidently a race they commonly play)

TRUGANINNI: Keep up or get left in the dust, shorty!

(...and motors off, cackling)

TRUGANINNI: Look out, Hobart!

NANNA: *(struggling to catch up)* Hey, you stick to the rules!

TRUGANINNI: Road rules, m'bum!

(After a few rounds of being left behind, NANNA gives up breathless)

NANNA: Rules... rules.

TRUGANINNI: *(calling ahead)* Outa the way or die a tragic death!

(They skylark a bit more until soon tired out.

LEVEY comes forward again. He is still with them in spirit but in now front stage addressing the audience again – and if he engages TRUGANINNI or NANNA in conversation it is from over-the-shoulder...)

LEVEY: But don't get me wrong. It was a good room, that. Not all musty n' heavy talcs. Y'could say it were perfectly *theirs* in its room-to-move... old Alexander Maccie made a name for himself out o' them but he always had a lot o' empty spaces about him; am I right or a rorter?... and it brightly opens out onto his front garden all bobby dazzler with flowers. Given Hobart, that'd be the alpine type.
   (small pause)
The thing was, when you cocked it, there this 'ere something out of place -- a blood'n'bone sort of taint, like you get around the lion cages at the zoo. Or the bathroom when me missus's at home, ha ha. If they'd had any bar of me bein' there, I would 'ave said let's throw open them Frenchie windows and let something a bit fresh

in. An' yours truly was no sooner thinking about this sniff-sniff when you can hear old Truganinni unwrapping this 'am sandwich which she had had to 'ave scrounged from the kitchen, as I live:

> *(He directs audience attention back to the women. There, yes, TRUGANINNI is gleefully unwrapping a ham sandwich while NANNA is extracting something that is obviously their secret from the cupboard. They are having a great and naughty-old time.*
>
> *TRUGANINNI has carefully extracted the meat out of the sandwich by the time NANNA returns to place a small goanna on the bed in front of them.*
>
> *Not seen so clearly, NANNA has gone to a cupboard and has pulled out something and put on bed before them both)*

LEVEY: An' as I live they were going to what I thought was to that there sandwich there:

TRUGANINNI: Ooo's my pretty little boy?

NANNA: Ooo's our own widdle Billyboy?

TRUGANINNI: Ooo's eating his greens and putting hair on his chest, then?

NANNA: Ooo's called Billyboy or your Majesty will do, then?

LEVEY: An' it was no sandwich, I'm tellin' yer. It was this 'orrible great man-eatin' lookin' lizard, ugh. Makes me shudder still; can't stand the sight of call-'em-goannas-I-don't-care, never 'ave.
   (listens, then shouts back to louts in audience)
Oi, don't be like that! I'll 'ave yer know, I married me ball'n'chain cos she 'ad herself covered up. Her puckers ain't nowhere near that thing's puckers. Not then at least.

TRUGANINNI: Ooo wants a tickle, itchy itchy coo?

NANNA: Ooo's our one'n'only 'andsome Billyboy, then? Ooo's growing a moustache?

LEVEY: (carries on) Not like this, nuffin' in me life was. They had this 'ere yellow ribbon tied round its great 'orrible purple neck with this 'normous bow. It 'ad on little red pants they 'ad knitted with a hole for that revoltin' tail. On its back'n'sides they had painted faces with smile on 'em. Straight up, that. An', listen to this, mind, on its head they 'ad tied a sailor's cap like old Bill would 'ave worn.
   (*back at louts at back again*)
Oi, weren't nuffin like me wife's wedding outfit!

TRUGANINNI: (chucking it under the chin, crooning) Billy boy, Billy boy…

NANNA: Ooo's got muscles where he-men ought?

LEVEY: Muscles. It 'adn't moved a blessed one! It was just sat there with that slice of 'am hangin' 'alf out of its disgusting purple-lips o' a mouth, like it 'ad an eternity to wait for a bit o' audience appreciation. An' I can tell you that takes a lot o' eternity to wait for. They tell me the real King Billy, he came to not move much either. Did that matter to old Truganinni or that other? Not that I could see. It was like they were so 'appy that old Bill was alive again.
   (*then*)
The way they 'ad it so secret, there was no way Alexander McKay knew about it. Then they just sit back with their backs to the window and smile and there's Kingboy there not movin' a revoltin' purple thing like 'e's surveying all he commands. Then they start arguing about who's allowed to go the hole or sumthin'. One says she want to and the other says she wants to so the other can't go, an' so on whatnot. Got me confused, I tell yer. So I think to m'self I'd better buzz off or make m'self known again as a deep thinker to them again. So I ups an'…

   (*He calls back to them overshoulder*)

82

LEVEY: 'Ere, Truganinni missy, say if life itself dropped in for a cuppa tea, what would you say to it, in a face-to-face way?

TRUGANINNI: I'd say 'Suck on this'.

NANNA: I'd say 'One or two spoonfuls?, hey, use the fork we got issued with!'

TRUGANINNI: I'd say 'One or two spoonfuls?, use a bit of bark like we had to'.

NANNA: Who'd he say wanted to drop in for a cup of tea?

TRUGANINNI: Life.

NANNA: Life? That rotten b.!

TRUGANINNI: Tell the rotten b. to stand in line like all the other lover-boys have to!

NANNA: Yeah!

LEVEY: I hadn't seen her for forty nigh years, but making conversation was obvious gettin' me nowhere. Anyway, there's this…

    (A polite knock on the door)

LEVEY: It was obviously McKAY comin' back. Don't ask me why but I didn't want him to see I was still in their room an' it was like trying to step into a boat without bringin' up dinner. I decide to pop out of the frenchie doors, go round the back and pretend I was just lookin' round his garden while he was in the kitchen, like.
    (and)
An' it's wot I did too. I slip those frenchies open an' step out into the garden an' suddenly I'm hearin' them two screechin' blue murder behind me. I whip around to see what's up and there's the purple monster off the bed and movin' alright. Cripes, I thought it

83

was attackin' me and who wouldn't? So I take off, screechin' up a bit o' blue murder m'self and for a time I hear that purple monstrosity closin' in and feel that purple tongue horror wrappin' around my delicates, until I look back an' it's just disappearing over the front wall. Well, it were my words against theirs with McKay so I decided to go out the back gate and go about me business. I didn't even stop to look around as to how many heart beats I'd dropped, I don't mind tellin' yer.

    (He flourishes)

LEVEY: An' that's a blackout on that.

    (Blackout, except for a spotlight on LEVEY at front stage.

    In solitary light, he lights up a cigar, puffs away for a bit, then takes a bite of a sandwich)

LEVEY: (shows cigar then sandwich) This one's for old Billy, and this one's for that purple monster, since we're here for the tributes.
    (*then*)
That were the first time I saw the old girl in nigh on forty year, an' she near sent me purple with a 'eart attack!
    (*back to some loutish comment*)
I 'eard that!
    (*then*)
A couple o' weeks after that… me still down there buying up all the seal skins to cover m'self from freezin' from being down there… I get this 'ere second note from McKay. In it, he says some 'kind' soul threw the purple nightmare's body back over the wall and into the front garden the next day an', while it were news to him, it affected the old gal 'ard, he says, an' I'd be very welcome if I could spare the time to pop in an' cheer her up, if I weren't too purple m'self from the cold. There was more to it too… but, 'ere, we'll show you…

    (A moment before lighting returns to the room and before he turns to join McKAY being as stern as he can to

TRUGANINNI and NANNA.

There is a noticeable change in the two women now.
TRUGANINNI is sunk back sitting on the floor in a corner.
She looks like a fallen rag doll, lifeless.

At her feet lies the body of Billyboy.

NANNA is kneeling by her, stroking her hair)

McKAY: (low and sad voice to TRUGANINNI) Haven't we always looked after each other?

TRUGANINNI: (surprisingly, but into air, almost in lullaby) A ridge of sand and animal droppings.
   (*mutters on*)

McKAY: (to NANNA) What did she say?

NANNA: She said, 'If it was only me, I would dance on an empty belly'.

McKAY: (encouraged) Try to walk.
   (*motioning NANNA to help raise her*)
Come on, old girl.

   (TRUGANINNI actually allows herself to be lifted. But, when she is almost to her feet, she sees some shadows fall across the window.

   People outside are obviously crowding around and trying to look over the wall. In fearful fright, she collapses back)

TRUGANINNI: Aiee…!

   (NANNA goes furiously to the French window

   NOTE: throughout this final scene, shadows outside the window appear trying to stare into the room. As shadows, they grow larger, more insistent)

NANNA: HERE, YOU TAKE OFF OR YOU'LL COP THE SLOPS!

TRUGANINNI: (rocking) Oi... oi...

(CROWTHER comes in. With his medicine bag, he has obviously answered McKAY's call)

CROWTHER: Spare the slops here, Nanna, it's only me.

McKAY: Thank God you've come, William!

(LEVEY and CROWTHER nod greetings. CROWTHER turns to find TRUGANINNI shrunken back into the corner with 'KING BILLY's' body. She is now trembling badly.

One look at her, and he simply puts his medicine bag aside as useless)

CROWTHER: So what's the trouble today, m'lady?
  (gets no reply)
Don't you mind those crowds outside. It's only because of fame'n'fortune, lucky you. Ask Mr Levey here.

LEVEY: (trying to inject humour) They build up anymore I might buy their crowd rights off yer!

McKAY: (urgingly to TRUGANINNI) They know you're safe in my house. Stand up and let them see you safe and well here.
  (finding it there)
Here, the red handkerchief you always wear outside.

CROWTHER: I don't think that'll be needed, Alexander.

LEVEY: (aside to audient) Cor, even I could see that.

TRUGANINNI: (finally) What do you want from me, white man?

86

CROWTHER: (rather surprised) What do I want?

NANNA: She was speaking to him.

>   *(she points to McKAY)*

CROWTHER: (censorially) I think you mean 'sir', not 'him'.

>   *(McKAY has to break the awkwardness that comes from NANNA refusing to recant what and how she said it)*

McKAY: For you to get better, Truganinni. In my house, there's no reason for you not to, is there?

>   *(As though in answer, TRUGANINNI starts humming)*

McKAY: (getting upset) On your life, are we running you down here?

NANNA: 'Ere, she always wanted to be outside, not inside.

McKAY: She did not!

NANNA: (now really standing up for her) She did.

McKAY: Never!

NANNA: Nobody listens anymore.

TRUGANINNI: In the night, the fire would be lit, but there would be the whisperings. Whisperings, whisperings, the shadows from the north.

>   *(The shadows swell again; voices become audible again)*

TRUGANINNI: (outcry) Don't let them in!

McKAY: Don't give up or I'll have to!

(NANNA calms her down as best she can, stroking both TRUGANINNI and the goanna)

NANNA: Here. Here.
  (pointing Billyboy's body)
They didn't have to do this.

LEVEY: (piping up despite himself) That's what I say when I meant it should be covered up.

(The other two men stare daggers at him)

LEVEY: Sorry bout that. Slipped out.

McKAY: (to CROWTHER) My house… everyone knows there's no reason for her not to get better.

CROWTHER: (low voice) We could move her into the hospital.

McKAY: No… no. It has to be here.

TRUGANINNI: (surprisingly strong burst) My legs were not strong enough to keep them away, Father. My mother speaks to you in this is a dark and waterless place.

(McKAY pushes past CROWTHER to speak intimately to her)

McKAY: (self-pity) I didn't have to…
  (stops and starts again)
Truganinni, I didn't have to carry on with your people. You know that. You were there. You must know I didn't join the Robinson just to send you all to that island. Nobody can say I did that,
  (pause)
But then, who's going to say I didn't? Would you? Would you go outside, right now, and tell them that? Truganinni?

TRUGANINNI: (outcry) Don't let them cut me up!

McKAY: (losing his composure) Whatever you're trying to do...
DON'T DO IT IN MY HOUSE!

(TRUGANINNI cries out something again)

McKAY: What did she say?

NANNA: (a fighting cock) She said, '*Bury me behind the
mountains!*'

*(McKAY stares down at TRUGANINNI, bypassing NANNA
as much as possible.*

*TRUGANINNI stares back at him as defiantly as she is able
to. It seems to drive her to get to her knees without much
help from NANNA.*

*When there, she collects the body of Billyboy in her arms
and walks on her knees out through the French windows,
cradling it in her arms.*

*In the garden plot just outside, she starts using her bare
hands to dig a grave.*

*When NANNA sees what she is doing, she sobs aloud and
drops down to join TRUGANINNI to, too, use her bare
hands to dig.*

*There is a silence... but a heavy one... while the two women
bury the body.*

*When they have finished, NANNA helps TRUGANINNI back
inside, where the latter at least allows NANNA to settle her
in the wheelchair and not on the floor in the corner.*

The men watch her doing so without moving.

Particularly with McKAY, it is a defiant gesture from her

which does not go unnoticed. He turns to appeal to CROWTHER, who only shrugs back 'what-to-do?'.

Shaking his head that this is all unfair, he turns to CROWTHER and LEVEY...)

McKAY: (appeal) William? Barnett?

(Both other men merely give back a sympathetic shrug.

LEVEY sees the impasse and how it is time to turn back to the audience by walking slowly back to the front apron of the stage:)

LEVEY: I don't know exact what Maccie was on about, but, straight up wit' you, I was sorry to see all that.

(McKAY strides from room. CROWTHER, with nothing much he can could, follows him out.

NANNA makes sure TRUGANINNI is as comfortable and rugged up as can be, then hurries over to the sideboard)

NANNA: Wait, wait.

(She returns to TRUGANINNI with a bowl of soup. This she places on a tray on her lap. She stands by her side and (this time gently) prods her with a bony finger)

NANNA: Soup, soup.

(TRUGANINNI doesn't take it.)

NANNA: (will never give up) Soup.

(When it is obvious that TRUGANINNI is not going to drink, her shoulders slump in hopelessness. Finally:)

TRUGANINNI: Don't you cry

NANNA: Who's crying?

TRUGANINNI: Don't you cry.

NANNA: 'Ere, why would I be crying?

TRUGANINNI: (no heart in it) Dopey.

NANNA: You, dopey.

TRUGANINNI: (no heart in it) Dopey.

NANNA: (ditto) Dopey.

> *(Lighting fades from them.*
>
> *LEVEY re-emerges front stage for the audience, and…)*

LEVEY: Now 'ere's the real sad part, yer could say. See, I got to see old Truganinni one last time after that. It were like this… I was wharfside an' 'ad just taken the directions to get to me ice-breaker of just follow the icicles, when Maccie's last call came, come quick. Well, I got to 'is place in five minutes flat, four of 'em taken up getting out o' me outer layers.

> *(He walks back to the 'play area' to join TRUGANINNI and NANNA… where the lighting-up has NANNA is trying to make the lifeless TRUGANINNI take tea.*
>
> *It is as he will describe while he stands behind TRUGANINNI's wheelchair, with his hands on its head rest…)*

When I got there, what I saw would break yer heart. See, on the way I learnt them Hobartians 'ad come to learn about the old girl investin' purple Billyboy with the attributes, like, of King Bill in the flesh, but also what the buggers'd done to 'is body them five years before.

(*pause*)

Yer wouldn't believe this, but this time old Nanna's on her old knees again by old Tru's side, who's drooped over her wheelchair like one o' them rag dolls, an' she's gently prodding this cup of tea at the old girl over and over all dead hopeless goin' with each dead-hopeless prod, 'Tea. Tea. Tea. Tea….' Not soup this time. Tea. Bless me, I dunno why it matters. Tea. Tea. It sounds like it does.

(*actually has to gather himself*)

See, the thing is some effer 'ad dug Billyboy up. Some effer 'ad chopped off his revoltin' purple little tail and left it there by the grave they dug with their own bare hands out the frenchies there. Some rotten sod 'ad had chopped off his revoltin' purple little head and left it there by his little grave old Tru and her Nanna'd dug out with their bare hands like it were one o' the great gorges of the Franklin River they got down there, frozen over 'alf the time. Some rotten sod 'ad lopped off his revoltin' little legs and left them there by the little grave they'd dug out of the great ochre plains of the Outback, like as if. See, some dirty muck 'ad cut off the smilin' face they 'ad painted on his scaley purple 'orrible-looking little back an' let the patch o' skin lyin' there plain as day by that grave. But no one had left his revoltin' little purple monstrosity of a torso there… oh no… an' there's this revoltin' trail of purple uck blood goin' off across the garden and over the wall. Greasy as some of m'smiles.

(*and*)

This I seen with me own eyes. Put them out! Am I a thinker or a blinker? Only is left old Tru shrunk now to that chair like that rag doll and old Nanna croonin' to her: 'Tea. Tea. Tea…'

> *(He leaves TRUGANINNI and NANNA and comes forward to front stage and to the audience again.*
>
> *As he comes the lighting fades behind him until he is left front stage with his own spotlight again)*

LEVEY: This is the last time I saw the old girl. I'm tellin' yer, it was like near the end of time. All what rumblin' down to me now is 'Tea, tea' and 'Don't cry' an' 'Who's cryin'', over'n'over, enough to burst your 'eart strings, you know? At the end of old Tru's eyes are trapped tears or maybe the hard shafts of the outside streamin' in. They say as old extinction is forever, give or take a day. What do I know?

(There is a long pause which could actually be the end. But LEVEY is just playing the showman again:)

LEVEY: Oi there, before you choof off. Old Alexander McKay, seems he weren't in time to get the old Tru's story like he said, but he did get the story of that other one, that Nanna, an' he didn't even charge me pretty penny to buy it.
(flourishes for, and gets, drum roll)
What's going to knock yer for six, is we're bringin' it to yer. We are! Am I a liar or on fire?
(out to louts at back)
That'll be enuff out o' you lot! Hose down yer own pants!
(carries on)
But, that ain't all the gubbins… ain't this Barnett Levey & Sons of the Royal after all?... what we can bring yer now is the story she *wanted* to write. How's that at no extra charge?!

(He pulls out a few sheaves of paper to read from)

LEVEY: Now, accordin' to what's rehearsed, what I'm goin' to do is read a few lines to show it's straight up an' then I'll let 'her' take over. No need to give 'er a hand, just give her a few minutes'll, eh?

(He starts out reading the first few lines…)

LEVEY: *'So they closed down the Mission. What to do? I get to the dock where they're bringing in all those single men and I hitch up my skirts and I showed a bit of leg and I stand on that there wharfside and I shouted, 'Right any of you lot, who's game?' Not one stepped forward. What a bunch of Gutless Wonders. So I'm there alone on this bush track out of Hobart like a shag on a…'*

(NANNA walks on, takes the sheaves of paper from him,

carries on reading from them as necessary. It is as
continuous a monologue as possible and almost chanting...)

NANNA: *'... a rock when suddenly there's Tru gunning steam*
outa twin spoilers as she pulls over the Shag Magnet. She traded
that stupid old wheelchair up for a Wheelchairs-r-Us Shag Mobile
mean machine with two copper boilers that'd bust your mainstays
boiling away and red'n'black trim and matching cow guards and
no less than three gears to make choofing up Mt Everest seem like
going downhill or what? Hop on, old Tru says. No worries, I say.
Halfway across Bass Strait on the crest of the biggest brute of a
wave you'd ever see, I get up the nerve to ask her, How come
we're hitting the mainland? Old Tru yells back, Van Diemens
Land can eat my fanny's honey flow. But we only just past
Flinders Island when old Tru gets wind of Bill down there hauling
in this whale, bleeding all over their precious boats and precious
wharves and precious streets, and in a heart's beat, blow me, but
Tru's going all lovey-dovey and bringing the Shag Mobile down
alongside his boat, even diving down twenty fathoms to save his
false teeth from hitting the bottom, with these stars coming out of
her eyes and batting her eyelids calling Ahoy you can come
alongside me anytime, you hunk o' meat you. Hop on Bill, she
shouts. No way Ugly, he belches rum back, but she was a goner
right from the start, a real pushover. So we end up choof-choofing
around that Bass Strait in the wake of old Bill's boat like a
lovesick seagull, her not me. Me, I'm there worrying more about
the poor Shag Mobile's paint job. Next thing I know she's tailed
him ashore at Hobart Town, George Town, Queenstown, and all
them other towns, and she's hardly let go of the steam valve let
alone touch the brakes, that's how much she wouldn't let him out
of her sight. He couldn't stagger out of a Ladies' Lounge without
old Tru's waiting outside and letting him flake out over the
shopping basket and gunning the Shag Mobile up'n'down all their
streets like it every night was the Easter Parade not drunks-night-
out, and honking away MAKE WAY FOR KING BILLY, ME
ONE'N'ONLY because that's what they were coming to call him
too, King Billy, on account he's supposed to be the last breeder
instead, far as I was concerned, the last bleedin' no-hoper. So
we're doing all those point-of-eight wheelies down their white-

arsed streets in the middle of the night, like King Billy was a right old Lord Muck of the Fowlhouse and the Sailor's Rest was some palace not the local doss house. Only that time when the real la-di-dah Prince of Wales sails up to meet him on board the real royal yacht does he get on the right side of the law. Even that time with the Prince of Wales, he turns up blotto and falls over the side and there's us in the Shag Mobile fishing him out of the drink by the seat of his pants with a gaff. So there's old Tru starting to crying'n'sighing because what can we do for the drunken sod? We rode those whale backs so he wouldn't have to strain his harpoon eye. We towed their carcasses back to the mother ship so the lazy b. wouldn't get splinters rowing himself. Even in the teeth of the great Southerlies, you could hear his mates all sniggering, Bloody old Bill's got a bit of a black pitch on the side. It tore my heart out, that. If you listened right you could hear old Tru bleeding inside, going, He's the last man for me, ever! And me trying to reason with her, He is the last, Tru. And she screaming back, What's the time lag, dopey? And I'm saying, 'How many letters?' but don't ask me why. What can I say you ain't heard? Tru, she bawled her eyes out after they found old King Bill, big celebrity by then, stiff as a board. At the hospital, they stole his skull and after that the government mob sawed off his hands and feet and after that they find her Bill gone from his grave, robbed like it wouldn't happen to a dog and leaving just this trail of blood. And I point at that empty hole in the ground and I say to old Tru, that's your map of your Van Diemen's Land right there. Does it make it any better for Tru? No sir. She guns the Shag Mobile along that left blood trail there to find her Bill, but what she don't know I know is they're now after her too with them calipers. I'm even up there on the Shag Mobile's spokes trying to beat them off, but they kept coming like flies. I don't give a shag, I want my Bill, old Tru yells. But I felt her grab me close and I felt her shivering and god almighty it was like the quivering of the heart of a sigh, 'Bury me out of the way!' Oh dear. Oh dear. I pushed her back onto the Shag Mobile and I take the wheel and I put my foot down and gunned us up the incoming tide of the Derwent right out through the heads out there, then we rocketed right up into the biggest sunset you'd ever see. At up where heaven starts and we end, I levelled the Shag Mobile out and we put our heads down and we slept the sleep of the innocent up there at Zero G for, what?, maybe 10 or 20 of that new Australian-English Ashes series until one day she shooed off the family of wedgetails that'd made their nest in the Shag Mobile's footboard, talk about taking a liberty. Then she worked up a real head of steam again, right hand down, back down we rocket to this same Earth. Stand aside, World, I'm coming through!, old Tru's shouting again all refreshed and up to her old tricks again. Talk about a couple of gay strumpets on the loose again! We caught this dirty great tsunami and we hung ten and tubed and nailed the break right across Flinders Island and we freestyled right across the beach at Port Fairy, up the main drag past the library, over the Grampians, up through the Wimmera to the River Murray flats through the orchards and plonk farms and onto the Central Aussie Desert and a turn or two around Burkie's and Willsie's ghosts, hammered along with a wurly-wurly to nail something they said was one day going to be Our Opera House, with a few scorching wheelies, flew through the Great Dividing Range, thumbing our noses at their calipers and skull-stealing tricks, burned off the crocs up Far North way, did a two-wheeler of a U turn burning those rims, then touched down light as a flibberty feather, three-point landing, neat and nice, right on top of Ayers Rock at sunset time. Lovely, it was. Uluru, Truggie sighed. Oo-roo to you too, I sighed. Doper, she said. Safe at last. Spot on at last. Basked in ruby were we, I tell you, her and me, silly old molls. We spun in the swoon of the great rock's eve-tiding, its amethyst in-swathed. When the great Tasmanian wolf hooted at the drunken boson moon, we lay the evening of our lives down in it and you should have my Tru's dreamings of huge coilings, immense gorgings, hummings-along in the all-of-times of the great Rainbow Serpent, in the never-never evers and themthere river beds, and I'm telling you how there were the everlastings there and the gay-lauds of all the tribes as all sparks flibberted moon-wooed up and flittered over and over and over all. Then suddenly old Tru softed and I heard such a shoofty. She vibrated and shook me and nodded and let off the Shag-Mobile's triple-bypass, and on the top of the Great Rock she's going, 'Got here finally'. and I say, 'Where's finally-here?', and Tru just points down and says and said 'Here at Billyboy, where've found him again, dopey; isn't he coochie?' You can believe this or not. Then all she has to do is lean out over the driver's side and pick our King Billyboy up from the running board. Proud as punch, she and our Billyboy was, his widdle purple neck already cocked for the scratchy-scratchies, and she's clucking, 'Oo's my Sir King Billyboy then?' What a laugh my Tru's got on her! I tell you. They didn't make me a quarter caste and inside for nothing, right? What can I say but, where was I? So Tru stokes up the Shag Mobile again here we go towards the far horizon. Where to now?, I shouted into the slipstream and into the wind in her hair when she had her long curls. She was laughing at last and I heard her shouting glee, 'We're going where the ham sandwiches are the best with not a scalpel slice in 'em, bloom and blush hush-a-bye Australia's land can!' And when we got our Billyboy back to Hobart town, die-soon, in out dust, I remember going: Take tea, I said. Don't let them cut me up but bury me behind the mountains, she said, bury out of the way. Drink tea, I said. It's only tea. It's free. Don't let them cut me up but bury me behind the mountains, oh. Take tea. Tru. Queen Tru. That's a good girl, that's all I can say.

> *(She finishes and just stands there staring outwards. LEVEY comes to her, points her towards the wings and pats her to go.*
>
> *Now he is in his own last spot. He is looking very old. He speaks 'solitarily' and, for him, very seriously to audience:)*

LEVEY: Okay it was more than five minutes. Any of you still 'ere?
   (*and*)
I am. I am. I never thought I would be either.

(End)